Tournament Poker:

101

Winning Moves

Expert Plays for No-Limit Tournaments

Mitchell Cogert

[handwritten inscription] CARLA – Play poker or just win! Mitchell Cogert

Tournament Poker: 101 Winning Moves
Expert Plays for No-Limit Tournaments

By Mitchell Cogert
© 2008 All rights reserved
ISBN: 1434892220

Published by CreateSpace
www.createspace.com

Design by Nu-Image Design
www.nu-images.com

For additional information go to www.apokerexpert.com

Table of Contents

3

How To Put This Book Into Action **194**

The Main Event:
You Versus A Champ Named Phil

Know the Moves to Improve Your Results

Do you lose poker tournaments because you don't always know the right plays?

Tournament poker is a fun way to win big money and become famous. The problem is that no one is willing to share the moves that made the top poker pros millionaires.

And yet, there is an incredible amount of information available. If you Google search "poker tournaments" you will get 2,650,000 results. If you Google search "no-limit tournaments," you'll hone this list down to a meager 527,000. That's quite a long list of books, articles, blogs, web sites and videos about poker.

And, that's the problem. There is just too much poker material, and with too many plays scattered all around. There isn't enough time for you to dig through all of them.

Ideally, it would be great to have one reference book where you can have all the best moves right at your fingertips.

Tournament Poker: 101 Winning Moves is the one poker book that you will want to keep nearby as an invaluable reference to know all the expert moves to improve your game and win no limit tournaments.

Tournament Poker: 101 Winning Moves gives you one hundred and one expert plays for no-limit tournaments. It is the poker reference book that combines winning poker moves found in almost 20 years worth of poker materials with plays uncovered in heads-up battles against poker pros Daniel Negreanu, Erick Lindgren, David Pham and others.

This book will put you on the fast track to success, as you will:

- Accumulate chips by using 40 pre-flop moves including the min-raise, the isolation play, the squeeze, the no-look bluff, and the position power-raise.

- Intimidate your opponents with 30 flop moves such as the continuation bet, the defensive bet, and learn to set a trap.

- Scoop the pot with over 20 turn and river moves like the delayed continuation bet, the action-inducing bet, scare card moves, and the naked Ace bluff.

- Walk away the champion with winning moves for your head-to-head battle at the final table.

You may know some of these moves, but I bet you don't know them all. And if you don't know them all, you are at a distinct disadvantage. It's time to step up to the poker table with confidence and an arsenal full of winning moves.

The reality is that you can win no-limit poker tournaments, and you can win them more often. And I know my book will help to improve your chances.

Good luck, and I hope you win your next no-limit hold'em tournament.

Mitchell Cogert 2008

Acknowledgements: In writing this book, I want to thank everyone who added value to the final product: my Mom, Dad, Robyn, Robert Linderman, Paula Weinstock, Virginia Harrison, and The Vegas Year Blog.

In No-Limit Tournaments Risk is Good

"It depends."

I'm sick of hearing every poker question answered with "it depends." "It depends" is just a cop-out by someone who doesn't want to be second-guessed. I want a real answer, and I want it now!

Winning poker doesn't "depend." Winning poker requires that you take action. Be aggressive. Be feared at the table.

Here's your mantra for No-Limit Hold'em Tournaments:

Risk is Good.

Now, repeat after me: "Risk is Good."

I can't hear you—shout it out—*"Risk is Good!"*

The biggest mistake a tournament poker player makes is to think he can simply outplay his opponent and expect to win. It doesn't work that way. This is not a cash game where time doesn't matter.

This is a tournament where time works against you, as it continues to eat away at your chips with bigger and bigger blinds and antes.

And there's also this thing called luck. Even if you have pocket Aces against pocket Deuces, you are going to lose one out of five times. And what if that one time is when your opponent has you covered with more chips? You are out.

The fact is that you can outplay your opponent and still lose.

No-limit holdem poker requires that you take action, take risks, and not sit back and wait for premium hands. You need to gamble. You need to accumulate chips.

You need to embrace the risk inherent in the game. You need to get so many chips, that you can handle a bad beat and still win.

Risk is good, because playing safe in tournament poker is a sure way to lose.

I learned this fact a long time ago.

Back in 2002, I was a cash game player who had entered a few no-limit tournaments, without much success. Still, I decided to take a shot at The Northern California Poker Championship hosted by the Casino San Pablo. A field of 138 showed up for the $10,000 first prize and a trophy. The buy-in was a "staggering" $300. This was before poker tournaments became mainstream and casinos routinely hosted events starting at $1,000.

In the early stages of the event, I found myself with pocket Kings. After being re-raised pre-flop, I managed to get all my chips in the middle with this monster hand. As I flipped over my cards, I was floored to find myself up against pocket Aces. It has to be nearly 12,000 to 1 for that to happen. Worse than that, if I lost this hand, I'd be out of the event in 116th place. (Later, I learned it's only about 22 to 1 against someone having pocket Aces when you have pocket Kings.)

The flop missed me, and the turn came up empty. I was ready to take my bad beat story to the rail when, boom - the King hits the river. The poker gods saved me, and gave me some chips to play with, too.

About 20 minutes later, the tournament director broke our table. The field was down to 94, and I had a decent stack. However, when I sat down at my new table, I immediately started bleeding chips. I couldn't catch a cold at that table, never mind a hand, and with every blind increase my stack continued to shrink.

I started to think about my game. I had read T.J. Cloutier's book on tournament play called *Championship No-Limit and Pot Limit Tournaments*, and followed his advice religiously, but it wasn't working. This tournament was turning out like all the others. At some point in every event, I'd eventually go card dead. Again, I watched my chip stack slowly erode. When I finally had a hand worth playing, everyone quickly folded when I raised—they knew I was playing ABC, predictable poker.

At that moment, I decided to change my game. If tight play wasn't going to work, I needed to be aggressive. I wanted to be perceived as strong, but not as a maniac. I decided that if I had any Ace, or a paint card in my hand, I would raise like I had pocket Aces. Regardless of my other hole card, I was raising. If I had any kind of hand on the cut-off, button, or small blind, I would raise like I had a monster.

My new style started to pay off. I was dealt J-2 and raised. Everyone folded. I waited a hand or two before another picture card was delivered. "Raise." I confidently pushed in my chips each time. Everyone folded again, and again. It was fun.

A few times, I did get called. Since I hadn't heard about the "continuation bet" I played "fit or fold" poker – if the flop hit me, I'd bet; otherwise my play was simply to check and fold.

Overall, my aggressive play picked up chips. My chip stack grew from $3,200 to $14,000, and I was the chip leader at my table.

As the field whittled down to 67 players, I was moved to a new table. When I sat down, I realized my chip stack put me in third place among all the players. I tried hard not to think about winning the event, since it would be a jinx. Instead, I focused on playing this new, aggressive style of poker.

My first hand at this new table was a Q-7. "Raise." Another player re-raised me. That hadn't happened at my last table. I folded.

Mt second hand, Q-4. "Raise." Another player moved all-in. I folded again.

My third hand, A-10. "Raise." D'oh, another player moved all-in. I folded.

I was getting spanked. My blind aggression was costing me, and I was back down to $5,000.

A tap on the shoulder from the tournament director told me I was moving. The timing was right, and I couldn't have been happier as she moved me back to my former table, into the same seat. My first hand at the old table, I raised with J-7 and everyone folded. I guess I should have appreciated the importance of my table image.

Just like before, playing aggressively added to my stack. I raised in the small blind with Q♠-J♠. The big blind called. The flop came A♥-K♦-7♣. I was first to act with a straight draw and two over cards. I figured that if the big blind had an Ace, he would've re-raised me pre-flop, so I made a pot-sized bet. The big blind stared me down for over a minute before he folded. Phew!

As my chips increased, the other tables began to disappear until I made it to the final table. I had one of the larger chips stacks, so I decided to slow down to make sure I was viewed as a tight player. Other players that had been eliminated stood nearby and watched the action.

Once the table got down to 6 players, I came alive. "Raise, raise, raise," I'd say over and over again. Without fail, smaller stacks would fold to my raises.

When we were down to 5, I realized I was the chip leader. I decided to keep the pressure on. I raised 4 pots in a row and didn't get called. The fifth time I peeked at my cards, K♠-K♥. "Raise."

The big blind didn't believe I could always have a hand. He sized me up, and moved all-in with K-9. I called, and dominated his K-9.

Gee, this style of play was a lot more fun than just sitting back and waiting for big hands, and more profitable too.

The blinds increased to $2,000/$4,000 and I was in the big blind. The small blind moved all-in for his last $6,000. I called the extra $2,000 with my 5-3 and hit a 3 on the flop. I won the hand, and we were down to 4.

The button circled the table and I found myself in the big blind again. Someone raised four times the big blind to $16,000. I called with K♦-J♣. The flop was Q♣-Q♦-2♥. I didn't think he'd have a Queen, so I bet. Without a second thought, he folded.

I now had $120,000 in chips, which was as much as all the other players combined! I sat back and watched as the small stacks went at each other.

It was finally heads-up, and I found myself facing a local tournament veteran. I checked his stack size and realized that he had the same stack size as me! My wait-and-see approach allowed him to collect all those other chips. I felt uneasy since I had no clue on how to play against just one player. I never played heads-up at a cash game, ever.

First hand, I got pocket 8's. I raised the $6,000 big blind to $20,000. My opponent paused and then pushed all-in for $120,000. We've been playing poker for 9 ½ hours and he wanted to decide the winner on our first hand? I looked at this guy and figured he was trying to muscle me off my hand. He

13

knows that I know that he has all the experience – and I guessed he was trying to exploit it. I decided he was weak so I pushed all-in.

He showed Q♥-10♣. Turned out he had a decent hand. I revealed my pocket 8's. As the dealer started to turn over the flop, I saw the window card…it's an 8! It's over. I win!

Risk is Good.

Two weeks later, I flew to Vegas and entered a $1,500 No-Limit event at the World Series of Poker®. Before the event started, Phil Hellmuth came by my table and stated, "This is the toughest starting table I've ever seen. Four players with bracelets."

Well, I know he wasn't talking about me. I looked around and recognized a couple of the Pros from *Card Player* magazine— 2001 Main Event Champion Carlos Mortensen, and 3-time bracelet winner John Bonetti. The other two I didn't know, but just their presence at the table intimidated me. I played tight. I waited for cards. And I got knocked out early in the event.

I learned a simple lesson: Play passive and lose. Play aggressive and win.

Risk is Good.

Tip: Knowledge is Not Power

Some players know that "Risk is Good." They start an event being aggressive and playing strong, but at some point in every tournament these players revert back to survival mode. They have the knowledge, but they don't have the power to follow through. It's not their fault. It's their basic human need to survive kicking-in. In a poker tournament, though, survival leads to death.

Don't be one of those players. Rid yourself of this survival instinct in no-limit poker tournaments. No one wins a race by sitting. But that's what you're doing when you wait for premium cards. That big hand doesn't come often enough, and when it does, you raise and all the other players fold.

Turn the knowledge of "Risk is Good" into winning your next no-limit tournament.

Pre-flop Moves: Should You Slowplay Premium Pocket Pairs?

1. Early in the event, limp with pocket Aces.

Let's say you are lucky and get pocket Aces early in an event. What should you do?

Your goal is NOT to just win the blinds. The blinds are too small to make a difference to the size of your chip stack. You're goal is to maximize your return with pocket Aces, while minimizing your risk. Manage your pre-flop action so you'll be against one or two players at the flop.

Example:

You get A♠-A♥ in a middle position. It is early in the tournament. The blinds are $25-$50. You have $2,000. Everyone folds to you. You just call. The player on the button and the player in the big blind call. These players have about the same number of chips as you. The pot is $175. You have risked $50, to potentially win around $6,000.

The flop is K♦-9♥-2♠. If one of your opponents has a hand like K♣-10♣, this hand could be a big win.

Example:

You get A♠-A♥ under-the-gun. It is early in the tournament. The blinds are $25-$50. You have $2,000. You are the first to act and call the big blind. You are hoping to get a raise to limit the competition. Also, if someone raises, you can re-raise when the action gets back to you.

Unfortunately, seven players call your bet. The pot is $375. Get ready to fold.

The flop is K♠-10♥-2♠. While you have pocket Aces, you have almost no chance of winning this hand. This flop has two cards in the playing zone (the playing zone is often defined as any card from 9 though Ace), with two cards to a flush, and two cards to a possible straight draw. In addition, someone may have limped in with a hand like 2♥-2♣, giving them a set.

While you may be frustrated that you didn't win with your Aces, you need to let it go. You need to learn to fold pocket Aces in these situations.

Example:

You get A♠-A♥ on the button. It is early in the tournament. The blinds are $25-$50. You have $2,000. A player in a middle position with $2,500 raises to $200. Everyone folds to you on the button. You have two choices:

1. Re-raise. If you re-raise, the most likely outcome will be that your opponent will fold. If he has a big hand like pocket Kings, he may re-raise and you can move all-in.
2. Call. Most players will re-raise; however, why not call and take some risk.

Example:

You get A♠-A♥ on the button. It is early in the tournament. The blinds are $10-$25. You have $2,000. Three players limp into the pot. You don't want to face too many opponents on the flop, so you raise. The pot is $110. You raise to $110. One player calls. This is an excellent situation for you to win a big pot.

2. *Early in the event, limp with pocket Kings and Queens.*

The goal with these hands is the same as if you had pocket Aces. You limp into the hand to maximize your return, while minimizing your risk. Again, you want to act in a way to compete against at most two players.

Of course, your risk increases as your hand weakens. For perspective, if you have pocket Queens, the flop will have an Ace or King almost 40% of the time.

Most players are not willing to take a chance when they get a premium pair. They hope their opponent has a big hand, so they can re-raise and take down the pot.

Tip: If You Are Not Confident in Your Hand Reading Ability, Don't Limp with Pocket Aces or Kings

It takes time and experience to read your opponents. If you are not confident in your ability, don't limp with these hands. It will get you into trouble if a player raises you on the flop.

Instead, you should raise and re-raise with these premium hands. The fewer the number of opponents seeing the flop, the easier your decision will be on the flop.

Tip: Do You Hate Pocket Jacks?

Pocket Jacks is one of the most difficult hands to play since a card higher than a Jack will flop over 65% of the time. Players will often declare, "I hate freaking Jacks!"

If you limp with pocket Jacks early in an event, it will be easier to get away from the hand. If an over-card comes on the flop, you can fold.

But, pocket Jacks are too vulnerable to be a limping hand. Raise with pocket Jacks to reduce the number of opponents, and play them carefully on the flop. If two over-cards appear on the flop, just fold and move on. If one over-card appears on the flop, well, be careful. You just have freaking Jacks!

Pre-flop Moves: How to Play Small to Medium Pocket Pairs

3. Early in the event, small to middle pocket pairs are made for calling.

It is very tough to win a no-limit hold'em tournament without hitting a set to a small or middle pocket pair. The reason is that you can win a big pot, as it's nearly impossible for an opponent to put you on a set. In fact, you want your opponent to have pocket Aces when you call with a hand like pocket fives.

The most important rule for these pairs is "no set, no bet." If you don't hit your set on the flop, you will fold. Catching a set or better on the flop occurs roughly one in eight times.

You goal with small to medium pairs is to maximize your return with the least amount of risk. You don't care how many players see the flop, but you do want to see a flop as cheaply as possible. The key question is this: How much are you willing to pay to see the flop?

The odds of flopping a set or better is 7.5 to 1, which means you won't be getting the pot odds to call a raise. As a general rule, you should risk up to 10% of your chips to see the flop. You may even be willing to risk more if your opponent's chip stack is deep; that is, he has a large chip stack.

Example:

You have 4♠-4♥ on the cut-off (one position before the button). It is early in the tournament. The blinds are $25-$25. You have $2,000. An early position player, with $2,500, raises to $100. It will cost you $100 to call, which is only 5% of your stack. Call and see the flop.

Example:

You have 8♠-8♥ on the cut-off. It is in the middle of the tournament. The blinds are $200-$400. You have $15,000. An early position player, with $25,500, raises the big blind to $1,600. It will cost more than 10% of your stack to call. However, the raiser has a deep stack for this stage of the event. Take a risk and call.

Remember: No set on the flop, no bet.

4. In the middle to late stages of a tournament, raise with small to middle pocket pairs.

In the middle to late stages of a tournament, the blinds can have a big impact on the size of your stack. In addition, players tend to get tighter as it gets later in the event.

Your objective with these hands is to win the blinds by getting everyone to fold, or to see the flop with minimal risk and maximum rewards.

Some players like to limp with these pairs throughout the event in order to see the flop cheaply. However, this is a weak play as the blinds and antes are worth stealing, and your odds of improving are not great. An example is if you limp with 6♠-6♣, you know that you will get at least one caller. Since the odds of at least one over-card on the flop is significant, you have really given yourself only one way to win; that is, to hit your set.

Don't be passive. You need to accumulate chips to win. Raise with these hands even in early position to win the blinds.

Example:

You have 6♠-6♣. It is the middle of the tournament. The blinds are $400-$800, and you have $17,000. You raise from an early position to $2,500. The player to your left, with $30,000, re-raises and makes it $10,000. Everyone else folds. What should you do?

The pot is $13,700. It will cost you another $10,000 to call. It is not worth it. Fold.

Example:

You have 6♠-6♣ in middle position. It is the middle of the tournament. The blinds are $400-$800. You are the chip leader with $40,000. In middle position, you raise to $2,500. The player next to you, with $30,000, re-raises to $10,000. Everyone else folds. What should you do?

The pot is $13,700. It will cost you another $7,500 to call, which is more than 10% of your stack. Even though your implied odds are good, why take the risk at this stage of the event when your opponent appears to be way ahead? Fold your hand.

5. In the middle to late stages of a tournament, re-raise with small to middle pocket pairs.

Re-raising with small to pocket pair is a power move that is high risk. Your objective of the re-raise is to put so much pressure on your opponent that he will fold his hand. This is a great play when you have not been involved in many hands, and your chip stack needs a boost.

Example:

You have 8♥-8♦ on the cut-off. It is early in the tournament. The blinds are $200-$400, and you have $6,000. You have not played a hand for a long time. As a result, your table image is most likely that of a tight player. A player in middle position, with $9,000, raises to $1,600. Everyone folds to you on the button. What should you do?

Calling is the worst option. Don't risk over 20% of your stack in hopes of hitting a set on the flop.

You should either re-raise or fold. The decision is based on your read of your opponent's hand, and how he views your table image.

Since a three or four times re-raise will leave you with few chips, you should move all-in.

Tip: How Much to Raise with Pocket Pairs from Deuces to Jacks?

Don't be predictable with your raises. And don't make a defensive raise, which is a bigger than normal sized raise that signals to your opponents that you hold a vulnerable starting hand like pocket Jacks. This play also makes your decision on the flop harder since you have committed so many chips.

Instead, think risk-reward. If you get a vulnerable hand, vary your play based on position. Raise by smaller increments in an early position, like 2.5 times the big blind. And, raise bigger in a later position.

Of course, you can simplify your bet sizes by always raising the same multiple of the big blind when you enter a pot. An opponent will not know if you have pocket Aces or pocket Deuces if you always raise the same multiple of the big blind.

Pre-flop Moves: The Isolation Play

6. In the middle to late stages of a tournament, use the isolation play with small to middle pocket pairs.

The objective of an isolation play is to make a wager so big that it gets other players to fold so you can be heads-up against one opponent. An isolation play can be used to isolate a bluffer, a maniac, or a player on a draw.

An isolation play is best when you have a hand that does better heads up, like pocket pairs. When you raise as an isolation play you need to make a large enough bet to force other players to fold.

Example:

You have 8♠-8♣ in middle position. It is late in the tournament. The blinds are $3,000-$6,000. You have $100,000. A player in early position with $20,000 moves all-in. A second player, with $120,000, calls this raise. What should you do?

You don't want to call since you would have to beat both players with your medium pocket pair. Since the second player did not re-raise, you can assume that his hand is not strong. The isolation play will get you heads-up against the all-in player.

Move all-in.

Example:

You have 3♠-3♣. It is the middle of the tournament. The blinds are $500-$1,000. You have $22,000, and you are in the big blind. Everyone folds to the button. The player on the button only has $2,000, and moves all-in. The small blind, with $18,000, calls for half a bet. What should you do?

Again, calling is not a good play since you have to beat two players with a small pair. You want to isolate yourself against the all-in player.

Move all-in.

Pre-flop Moves: The Min-Raise

7. The Min-Raise.

When you reach the middle of the tournament, you want to win the blinds without a struggle. Picking up the blinds is key in accumulating chips. The min-raise, which is a raise of two times the big blind, is a move that can win the blinds uncontested.

Example:

You have Q♠-10♠. You have $22,000, and the blinds are $400-$800. Everyone folds to you. You are in a middle position. What should you do?

If you call, you invite other players into the hand, and at the very least, you will see a flop. Also, if someone raises after you limp, you will have to seriously consider folding. A raise of three times the big blind will risk over 10% of your stack on a mediocre hand.

With the min-raise, you are hoping that the $1,600 bet will get everyone to think twice about entering the pot. Opponents may put you on a small pair, an Ace-x hand, or a premium starting hand.

The other advantage of the min-raise is that it is an excellent defensive bet. A player, who would raise if he was first in the pot, may play it safe and just call.

Do not make this move after a player has already called the big blind. A min-raise is not going to get this player to fold.

Also, do not make this move from the big blind after there are a few callers. The worst play in no-limit poker may be when the big blind opens up another round of betting with a min-raise. Even if the big blind has pocket Aces, a min-raise from this position will not get players to fold.

Tip: Play More Pots in the Early Stages

One way to accumulate chips is to see more flops early in the tournament. Since the bet sizes are so small you can take a risk with a wider range of hands. If you hit your hand, you can win big pots against your opponents who are playing more predictably.

For example, let's say it's early in the tournament. You have $5,000, and the blind are $25-$50. You call a raise with 7♣-5♣ on the button. The flop comes A♠-7♦-5♥. If your opponent has A-K, you have the potential to win a big pot.

When your stack size is big relative to the blinds, look to gamble more with your chips. Consider committing at least 20% of your chips to these speculative hands. Remember you are taking a small risk for a big reward.

Pre-flop Moves: The Under-the-Gun Steal-Raise

8. The Under-the-Gun Steal-Raise.

The objective of a steal-raise is the same as the min-raise, to win the blinds uncontested. Typically, a steal is when you have a hand that is not worthy of a raise in its own right, but you raise based on position, your table image, your opponents' table images, how often the players in the blind defend, and you hope that your opponents don't have a hand that is worth calling your raise.

The under-the-gun steal move is best when you are feared at the table and/or the players at your table are tight. Your opponents may realize that you don't have a premium hand, but they feel that you will outplay them on the flop. Of course, this is an advantage that the poker pros have against their opponents.

The first time I noticed this move was at a WSOP event. It was the middle of the event, and the poker pro, Erik Seidel was under-the-gun. He only had fifteen times the big blind. Erik raised three times the big blind, representing a premium hand to the other players. Everyone folded.

A round later, Erik made the same move and won the blinds again without a struggle. He made it look easy, as no one at the table wanted to play against him. At the time, I thought Erik had premium hands, but later I learned that this is a move pros use to help them accumulate chips and stay in front of the constant blind increases.

Erik's image is of a smart, tight player. The players at the table were tight and waiting for big cards. Combined, this allowed him to steal the blinds from a vulnerable position at the table.

Pre-flop Moves: The Position Steal-Raise

9. The Position Steal-Raise.

It is common knowledge that if you are on the button and everyone folds to you, you should look to raise and steal the blinds. By raising on the button, you only have to get the two players in the blind to fold. Of course, the blinds know that you may be stealing their chips, and not always believe you.

Starting at the middle of the tournament, you should extend your thinking and consider the position steal-raise from the cut-off and the power position (two positions right of the button). Again, your objective is to win the blinds by putting pressure on the players to your left to fold. In fact, your pre-flop raise will get more respect when it is not from the button.

If you get called by one of the blinds, you have a positional advantage against your opponent; that is, you will act last in all the following rounds. Having position against your opponents is very powerful as you can observe your opponents and their betting action before you make your decision.

As it gets to the later rounds of the tournament, players are more hesitant to get involved without premium hands and the position steal-raise is an even more effective move.

Tip: What is Table Image? Why is it so Important?

The playing style that a player has at the table is considered his table image. If an opponent has not played any hands for a long time period, he will have a tight table image. A player who enters many pots with a raise will have an aggressive table image.

It is important to try to determine the playing style of your opponents since it will improve your decisions. For example, holding A-Q is a stronger hand against the aggressive player than a tight player. The reason is that the aggressive player is entering many hands and probably does not have a hand as strong as yours, while the tight player will need a premium hand to enter the pot. As a result, raising the aggressive player is a smart play, while folding may be the right play against the tight player.

It is important to think about the table image you have created for your opponents. Importantly, you will find that not all of your opponents perceive your image the same way. As a result, your decisions against one opponent may differ against another opponent.

As a general rule, though, you want to play the opposite of your table image. If your opponent views you as never being able to bluff, it will be easier to make a play that will bluff him out of a hand. If your opponent views you as a maniac, you will be much more likely to be called or even raised to put you to the test.

Pre-flop Moves: The Position Power-Raise

10. The Position Power-Raise.

Unlike a position steal-raise, where the objective is to steal the blinds, a position power-raise is designed to win both the blinds and the additional money in the pot from previous callers. It's a very effective play as you represent a strong starting hand to all your opponents.

Example:

You have K♦-10♦. It is in the middle of the tournament. You have $20,000. The blinds are $400-$800. Two players limp into the hand for $800. The pot is $2,800. Everyone folds to you on the cut-off. What should you do?

A call is an acceptable play in this position, since you want to see a cheap flop. But this hand is going to be difficult to play on the flop. The limpers probably have hands around the same strength as your hand, or even better. The callers could have K-J, Q-J, J-10, A-10 and have you out-kicked if you flop any pair.

Instead of limping, try the position power-raise. Instead of playing your hand, play against your opponents' mediocre hands by raising. Your raise needs to be large enough to get everyone to fold. Therefore, with $2,800 in the pot, raise to $4,000. It will cost the limpers another $3,200 to call.

Unless one of the players behind you finds a premium hand, an $800 calling hand is rarely worth another $3,200.

What if a limper calls your raise? First, you need to put him on a range of possible hands that could call your raise. Second, you have the advantage of position. Third, you can use one of the flop moves in the next section to get him to fold.

Tip: Fear. Dish It Out. Don't Take It In.

Ask yourself the following question: Will your bet put fear in the heart and mind of your opponent? If it will create fear for your opponent, make that play. If not, is there a move that will?

If your opponent makes a bet that puts fear in you, ask yourself if that is true or false. Remember that fear is often referred to as False Evidence that Appears Real. Is he bluffing? Semi-bluffing? Calling your opponent's bet may slow him down, or raising his bet may make him hide in the corner.

Pre-flop Moves: The Leave-Something-Behind Re-Raise

11. The Leave-Something-Behind Re-Raise.

Everyone knows that a re-raise is more powerful than a raise. However, some re-raises are more threatening than others.

Example:

You have J♠-J♥. It's in the middle of the tournament. You have $9,000. The blinds are $200-$400. You are in middle position and raise to $1,400. You want to win the pot uncontested, especially since there is a good chance there will be an over-card to your Jacks on the flop. The next player starts to count his chips as if he is trying to figure out how much to re-raise.

In which of the following re-raises does your opponent have a stronger hand?

In one scenario, the player to your left re-raises by moving all-in for $9,000. A call puts all your chips at risk.

In the second scenario, the player to your left re-raises your $1,400 bet to $4,200. A call puts about half your chips at risk.

The answer is that in the second scenario your opponent most likely has a stronger hand. His re-raise signals a premium starting hand, possibly pocket Aces. By leaving half his chips behind the line, he is committed to moving all-in on any flop.

In the first scenario, the all-in bet is most likely A-K, since he wants to see all five community cards. Of course, he would prefer that you fold your hand. The all-in move puts you in a life or death decision; if you lose, you will be eliminated from the event.

There is an interesting psychology whenever you re-raise a player and leave even one chip behind the line. Your opponent's first reaction is always, "Why?" Followed by, "Does this guy know what he's doing?" Yet, your opponent will often believe that you have a monster hand and muck.

Example:

You have A♣-9♣. It is late in the tournament. You are in the big blind and have $60,000. The blinds are $1,500-$3,000. A player on the cut-off, with $70,000, raises to $10,000. Everyone folds to you. What should you do?

Your options are the following:
1. Fold: Why get involved? Lose your $3,000, and move on.
2. Call: Risk another $7,000 and hope to flop at least one pair.
3. Re-raise: Re-raise an amount that indicates a premium hand.
4. Move all-in: Put in the remainder of your chips.

If you know your opponent is overly aggressive and stealing, any re-raise will get him to fold. However, if he has a hand as strong as A-J, K-Q or pocket 10's, is there an amount to re-raise that will get him to fold?

If you move all-in, it puts maximum pressure on your opponent. He is risking most of his chips on his decision. He may believe you are putting on a move and call your bet.

If you re-raise, let's say to $40,000, you will be leaving $20,000 behind. This looks like a strange bet, as traditional wisdom is that once you've committed more than half your chips, you might as well move all-in. However, it looks like you have a premium hand and want action.

Pre-flop Moves: The Re-Raise Against Overly Aggressive Opponents

12. The Re-Raise Against Overly Aggressive Opponents.

If you play in the bigger buy-in events, you'll end up playing with the same players for a long period of time. This is an opportunity to take advantage of the overly aggressive pre-flop raisers.

The overly aggressive pre-flop raisers are easy to spot. They come in with a raise way too often. You can pick on these players and use them as your personal chip-ATM machine. Simply re-raise these players and they will fold. All you need is a little courage.

Example:

You have A♠-4♦. It is late in the tournament. You have $50,000 and are in ninth place with thirty players left. The blinds are $1,000-$2,000. A poker pro, with $80,000, is in middle position and raises to $8,000. The pro views you as one of those ABC players; meaning, you play in a predictable manner. Everyone folds to you in the big blind. What should you do?

You have 40 times the big blind, so you don't have to take any drastic action. However, this pro has been running over the table with his pre-flop raises. He can't always have a hand, right?

Your hand does not play well after the flop, so calling is a bad play, and you can always play it safe and fold.

However, if you re-raise to $30,000, your opponent will most likely fold.

This is an excellent way to add chips to your stack since these overly aggressive players can't always have a hand, and they will not want to get involved with a tight player whose re-raise signals a premium starting hand.

The mistake too many players make is to wait for a premium hand to re-raise. Unfortunately, those big hands don't happen that often.

Another move some players make is to just call when they have a strong hand. If they have a hand like A♠-10♠, they are afraid to play strongly, so they call instead. Unfortunately, they are going to miss the flop almost two-thirds of time.

Tip: Timing is Everything

Re-raising an aggressive player works, unless your opponent finds a monster starting hand. One method to "tell" if a player has pocket Aces is how he watches the action behind him after he raises. If you notice this player watching the action more intently than before, beware. He wants action.

Pre-flop Moves: The All-in Re-Raise Against the Poker Pro

13. The All-In Re-Raise Against the Poker Pro.

One of the challenges in major tournaments is playing against the poker pro. The pros are aggressive and raise pre-flop more than other players. They don't even need a hand to do this. In addition, they know how to outplay you on the flop, turn and river (something I hope to change with this book!).

It is interesting, but some poker pros will fold to your re-raise, while other pros will call your re-raise. The pros that call re-raises are very tough to beat because if they sense any weakness, they will outplay you.

The correct move against the top poker pros is not to try to continually outplay them. Instead, find your spots to move all-in and put on maximum pressure. Pros hate the all-in move pre-flop since it takes their skill out of the game. It also makes it easier for you since there are no other decisions needed.

Example:

You have A♠-10♣. It is late in the tournament. You have $40,000. The blinds are $800-$1,600. A poker pro who has been outplaying everyone at the table has $80,000. In middle position he raises to $5,000. Everyone folds to you on the button. The players in the blind are tight. What should you do?

Move all-in. Make the pro decide if it's worth risking half his stack.

There are players who are overly aggressive pre-flop and call re-raises. And, there are players who are overly aggressive pre-flop and fold to a re-raise. Try to take advantage of both types of players. You need to accumulate chips, and these players are opportunities to add to your stack.

Embrace the risk in the game.

Heads-up against David "The Dragon" Pham: The All-in Re-Raise against the Poker Pro.

It was March 2004, and the Moneymaker boom was just beginning. I entered a $1,000 No-limit event at the Reno Hilton, along with 250 others, all chasing a first place prize of $80,000. I played fairly well, had some luck, and ended up at the final two tables. However, once we were re-seated, things heated up as David Pham joined my table.

I hadn't played with David before, but I quickly learned how this two-time bracelet winner earned his nickname "The Dragon." Hiding behind dark glasses and a thin mustache, he took complete control of the table through intimidation. It seemed as if the only word David knew was "raise." If someone dared to re-raise The Dragon, he would simply call, and then outplay him after the flop. It was amazing.

Since David was sitting immediately to my right, his aggression was taking a toll on me. He raised my blinds three consecutive times from the button and small blind. I folded each time, patiently waiting to catch playable cards. While I waited, I saw my chip stack gradually moving to my right.

David continued to accumulate chips as the button worked its way around the table. Once again, as I sat in the big blind, everyone folded to David in the small blind. Without missing a beat, he raised my blind. I chuckled, asking, "Do you always have a hand?"

David was silent.

I decided it was time to take a stand and defend my blinds. My plan was to push back and re-raise with any two cards. I looked over at David, who had me out-chipped almost 2 to 1. I peeked down. A-10 suited. Calculations of pot-odds were whirling through my head when I looked over at David. I wasn't getting steamrolled to the rail. I stopped calculating, paused for a moment, and moved all-in.

For the first time, David appeared troubled. He thought, and thought, and thought. It would cost him half of his stack to call. Finally, he folded.

But losing one pot didn't stop this juggernaut's aggression. The next round, he tried the same move on me from the small blind. This time, I decided not to look, and pushed all-in. David folded again. Cool!

One more time around the table and it was folded back around to David. I'm prepared for another one of David's raises, but instead he called. What? That was suspicious. A super aggressive player limping instead of raising is a red flag.

I looked at my cards, A♦-Q♥. Should I move all-in again?

No, I didn't trust his call. I raised. David called.

I decided that no matter what, I was done with this hand. There's no way I was going to be trapped.

The flop was K♠-4♥-3♦. We both checked. The turn was 9♦. We both checked. The river was a 3♣. We checked it down.

David showed 2♠-2♣. He won. I laughed as I exposed my cards to him.

I learned that the only way to fight aggression at the table is with even more aggression. More importantly, I realized the only way to beat David Pham at the table is moving all-in against him. He is that good.

Pre-flop Moves: Take Advantage of the Bubble

14. Be aggressive near the bubble. Raise with a wider range of hands right before the money stages in a tournament.

The player who finishes on the "bubble" is the one who finishes one place out of the money. In fact, the time in a tournament where it gets close to the money is called the "bubble."

When players get close to the bubble they tighten up. After playing for hours or days, the last thing any poker player wants is to go home with nothing. As a result, players who had a good-sized chip stack take a big sized hit. And players who had a small sized chip stack are forced to act before they are blinded off.

The reason to enter a tournament is to win it. The big cashes are in the first three places. Yet, when players get close to the money, they tighten up their starting hand requirements. They are looking to fold, because they don't want to get knocked out before getting in the money.

While this is human nature it is also a major mistake. It should not matter to you if you just win a few dollars or finish on the bubble.

When it gets near the bubble, resist the urge to survive. Look to thrive rather than survive. Take advantage of the other players' fears of missing the money and loosen up your starting hand requirements and raise.

Example:

You have A♠-9♠. It is late in the tournament. There are only two players left who need to be eliminated before making the money. The blinds are $2,000-$4,000 with a $25 ante. You are low in chips with $52,000, and are in a middle position. The chip stacks of the players behind range from $40,000 to $80,000. Everyone folds to you. What should you do?

This is not a great hand in a middle position. Your stack is low with a little more than ten times the big blind. However, you know that your opponents have tightened up a lot in the last round. In fact, in the last twenty minutes not one hand has gone to the flop.

A raise to $12,000 should win you the blinds and the antes. If you get called you may have make a difficult decision on the flop; however, you should consider being aggressive on the flop and moving all-in.

Pre-flop Moves: When to Raise with Suited Connectors

15. Starting at the middle stages of a tournament, raise with suited connectors in position

Suited connectors are difficult hands to play at all stages of a tournament. Early on in an event, you want to see a flop cheap with these hands, and play against multiple opponents. Later in the event, they can be chip-burners, as you will most likely be getting the worst of it when you get called.

Starting from the middle of the tournament, use suited connectors as hands that can steal the blinds. Raise pre-flop, and try to accumulate chips uncontested. If you get called, you can get in a lot of a trouble or be faced with some tough decisions. Other times, you can get real lucky and flop a nice hand, like two pair.

Example:

You have 7♦-8♦. It is the late in the tournament. You are in the power position. The blinds are $2,000-$4,000. You have $74,000. Everyone folds to you. You raise to $11,000. Only the big blind calls. He has $110,000. The pot is now $24,000.

The flop is J♥-7♥-2♣. It's the right color for a flush draw, but the wrong suit. You do have second pair. The big blind bets out to $18,000. What should you do?

The big blind is a new player to your table, so you don't know how he plays. Does his bet mean he has top pair? Or does he have a pair in the hole, like pocket 9's? Or maybe he is betting his flush draw? Or maybe he senses you're weak?

A player who acts first has the opportunity to bluff before his opponent can bluff. It is "the right of first bluff." You don't know if your opponent is bluffing, and you were not able to steal the blinds. Therefore, it is best to fold. Another hand will be dealt. Promise.

Pre-flop Moves: An Easier Way to Play A-K

16. The two moves with A-K: Either "use it or lose it."

There is so much material written about the A-K, it can be overwhelming. Today, some players will just blindly move all-in with A-K, while other players are callers and hope to hit their hand on the flop.

The simple truths about A-K are as follows:
- It is the strongest drawing hand in no-limit poker, meaning if you hit the Ace or the King you will have the best kicker.
- You will only flop top pair or better about 33% of the time. That means your hand will not improve on the flop about 67% of the time.
- It is a slight underdog to any pair before the flop.
- It is a big favorite to any other A-x hand.
- It is an opportunity to double-up or a disaster that knocks you out of the event.

There is a simple way to play A-K. Either "use it or lose it." If you can "use it" to accumulate chips without taking the worst of it, then raise, re-raise or move all-in. If you can't "use it" with the expectation of being ahead, then "lose it." In no-limit poker, a good fold is a good thing.

Example:

You have A♠-K♥ It is early in the event. The blinds are $25-$50. You have $2,500. An early position player, with $2,000, raises to $150. What should you do?

The worst thing to do is to just call. Since you have a drawing hand, you don't want your opponent to see a flop.

Re-raise to $600. A re-raise can get your opponent to fold.

Example:

You have A♠-K♥. It is early in the event. The blinds are $25-$50. You have $2,500. An early position player, with $2,000, raises to $150. A second player, with $4,000, re-raises to $450. What should you do?

Again, a call is the worst play. Fold or raise.

One of these players probably has a pocket pair. The second player's raise may suggest he has a premium hand, possibly pocket Queens. Pocket Queens will be a 57% favorite against A-K. And it could be worse if one of the raiser's also has an Ace.

Can you use your A♠-K♥ to get this player to fold? Even if you move all-in, a player with pocket Queens is not going to fold. In addition, you don't know the strength of the original player's hand.

The risk is too great that you'll be taking the worst of it. A-K is still a drawing hand. Just fold.

Example:

You have A♣-K♣. It is late in the event. You have $50,000. The blinds are $1,500-$3,000. You are one away from finishing in the money. In an early position, you raise to $12,000. Everyone folds to the player on the button, with $200,000, who re-raises to $39,000. It is folded back to you. What should you do?

A lot of players are happy to just get in the money. Don't be one of those players. Tournaments are about winning. Forget about the bubble, and play to win.

You need to accumulate chips, and you may not have a better opportunity than with A♣-K♣. Move all-in.

Your opponent calls and shows A♥-Q♥. The Q♣ flops and you are knocked out. That's poker.

Example:

You have A♠-K♥. It is the middle of the tournament. You have $57,000 and are the chip leader. The blinds are $300-$600. You raise to $2,000. Everyone folds to the player on the cut-off with $24,400. He raises to $12,000. It is folded back to you. What should you do?

Your opponent is pot committed, so this hand is going to cost you $24,400 or about 40% of your chips. Also, you are the chip leader.

A-K is a "use it or lose it" hand. There is no reason to risk more chips in this situation. You only have $2,000 in the pot so don't make it worse by playing this hand. Just fold.

Example:

You have A♠-K♥. It is the middle of the tournament. You have $57,000 and are in 7th place. The blinds are $300-$600. You raise to $2,000. Everyone folds to the player on the cut-off with $39,400. He raises to $12,000. It is folded back to you. What should you do?

Unlike the previous example, your opponent is not pot committed. You can use your stack to get him to fold, especially since there are only a few hands your opponent can feel good about playing against your re-raise.

Move all-in and put the maximum pressure on your opponent.

Example:

You have A♠-K♥. It is the middle of the tournament. You have $20,000. The blinds are $200-$400. An early position player moves all-in for $3,000. Everyone fold to you in a middle position. You call. Everyone folds to the player in the big blind with $15,000. The big blind moves all-in. What should you do?

Unfortunately, this is what happens in tournaments. You think you made the right play, and now someone comes over the top putting the pressure back on you.

Did you make the right play by calling?

No. A better move is to raise and isolate the all-in player. A raise may have stopped the big blind from going all-in.

In any event, take the chip loss of $3,000, and wait for a better opportunity.

Tip: Domination Isn't All That Dominate in Poker

Players like to have hands that "dominate" their opponents. A dominated hand scenario would be when you and your opponent hold the same highest-ranking card, but you have the better kicker. A common example is the A-K versus A-Q. In general, in these types of situations the player with the better kicker is better than a 2-1 favorite.

Unfortunately, the word domination is a poor choice. Domination means you have control or power over someone. You don't have anything of the sort. You are going to lose almost one in every three heads-up battles when you "dominate" your opponent.

Does that sound like domination or just being a solid favorite?

Pre-flop Moves: Know These Button and Blind Plays

17. When everyone folds to you on the button, don't raise, just call.

It is common knowledge that if everyone folds to you on the button, you should raise to steal the blinds. Stealing blinds with raises from the button is considered a smart play since you only have to get two players to fold, and even if you get a call, you will have position on your opponents.

Next time everyone folds to you on the button, don't raise, just call. This is especially effective if you have already raised from the button a couple of times and stolen the blinds. Your call is going to worry the players in the blinds because it's a strange move. The blinds will suspect you have a premium hand. As a result, a bet on the flop will usually win you the pot.

The other advantage of a call is that if one of the blinds finds a premium hand, you can fold when he raises.

This is a move to mix into your game to provide some balance. You don't want to be predictable in your game.

18. Call raises from the big blind even with a drawing hand if the pot odds are favorable.

Some players will defend their big blind almost every time. And some players will look for a reason to fold their big blinds.

You should not be predictable in your play. If you are in the big blind, and get raised, determine if there is a reason to play the hand. Even a hand as poor as 8♣-6♣ can be an opportunity to accumulate chips, if the pot odds are right.

Example:

You have 8♣-6♣ in the big blind. It is early in the tournament. You have $4,000. The blinds are $50-$100. A player in middle position, with $3,200, raises to $300. Everyone folds to you. What should you do?

Don't fold your hand so fast. Look at the pot odds. There is $450 in the pot, and it will cost you $200 to call. You are getting over 2-1. These are actually not bad pot odds. If your opponent has A-K, he is about a 60% favorite. If your opponent has Q-Q, he is about an 80% favorite.

Your hand is not too bad, since it's a one gap suited connector. You have a comfortable chip stack as you have 40 times the big blind. And you have an opportunity to win a big hand if you hit your hand.

If you have been folding in the big blind every time, lean toward calling in this situation. You don't want to be seen as a player who routinely folds in the big blind to a raise as your more observant opponents are going to steal your blinds.

When you play in major events, you'll run into poker pros that are notorious for calling in the big blind with any two cards. The reason these pros make this play is not because they have a big hand, but because they believe they can outplay their opponent.

You need to observe which players will and will not defend their big blind. If you run into a player who defends, make a bigger raise than normal to give him lousy pot odds to call.

Example:

You have 10♣-6♦ in the big blind. You have $4,000. The blinds are $50-$100. A player in middle position, with $3,200, raises to $300. Everyone folds to you. What should you do?

This is the same situation, except your hand is lousy. Fold.

Example:

You have 8♦-7♦ in the big blind. It is late in the tournament.
You have $52,000. The blinds are $1,000-$2,000, with a $50
ante. A player in middle position, with $64,000, raises to
$4,000. It is folded to you. What should you do?

The pot is $7,500. It will cost you $2,000 to call. You are
getting almost 4 to 1. Even if your opponent has pocket Aces, it
is worth calling to see the flop.

*19. Folding to pre-flop raises from the small blind is generally
the right move.*

The small blind has the worst position in no-limit poker. Yet,
some players feel a need to defend their small blind since
they've already committed one-half of the big blind. They are
usually chasing rather than defending their blinds.

Example:

You have Q♦-9♠ in the small blind. It is early in the
tournament. You have $2,500. The blinds are $25-$50. The
player under-the-gun raises to $150. Everyone folds to you. The
pot is $225. It will cost you $125 to call. What should you do?

You are getting a little less than 2-1 on your call. However, you
have a bad hand in the worst position, against a player that made
a raise from upfront. Avoid trouble and fold your hand.

In addition, the big blind has yet to act. If he re-raises in this
situation, you'll be forced to fold. Of course, some players
magnify their mistake by calling the re-raise from the small
blind.

Don't get involved. Did you forget you are about to be on the
button?

Example:

You have Q♦-8♦ in the small blind. It is early in the tournament. You have $2,500. The blinds are $25-$50. The player under-the-gun raises to $100. Three players call the raise. The pot is $475. It will cost you $75 to call. What should you do?

You are getting more than 6-1 on your bet, which are excellent odds. While you don't have the best hand now, you can flop a big hand. This is an easy call.

20. The small blind steal-raise.

One of the interesting facts of tournament poker is that players are passive in blind versus blind heads-up situations. While the player in the big blind is suspicious of a raise from the button, he is more likely to respect a raise from the player in the small blind.

Take the initiative in the small blind. If you know the big blind is cautious in blind versus blind play, raise. Your cards don't matter. Just make sure that you raise an amount that will get the big blind to lay down his hand. And if you do get re-raised, just let go of your hand.

Example:

You have 7♠-2♦ in the small blind. It is the middle of the tournament. You recently joined the table and are not sure how the big blind plays. You have $6,000. The blinds are $200-$400. Everyone folds to you. The big blind has $8,000. What should you do?

Test him. Forget your cards. Raise to $1,800. The big blind won't like your raise, and may even suspect you are bullying him. But unless he has a hand, he will fold. After all, he doesn't know how you play yet.

21. The big blind steal-raise.

Sometimes you will be in the big blind where everyone folds to the small blind, and the small blind just calls. This call screams weakness. At best, the small blind has a mediocre hand and he wants to see the flop on the cheap.

You need to make a big raise. Do not call in these situations. When the small blind shows weakness, take advantage of it. If he calls your raise, you will have the advantage of position, but you need to be very cautious.

22. Re-raising the overly aggressive button stealer.

You are in the big blind. Everyone folds to the player on the button. He raises you. You have a bad hand, so you fold. The next time around, you are in the same position, and the same exact situation comes up. When the button raises, you look at your hand and find J♠-4♣. You fold.

The third time around, same situation, and the button raises you again. What should you do?

At this point, your cards don't matter. Re-raise this player big and make him lay down his hand. You can't allow any player to push you around. And, you can't let other players at the table think they can run over you. If you do, you will be toast.

When you act aggressively even once, you will get the button's attention.

23. Move all-in when you have ten or more times chips as your opponent in the blind.

When you have overwhelming chip dominance against your opponent, don't just call. Specifically, anytime you have ten or more times the number of chips as your opponent, move all-in. It puts maximum pressure on your opponent, with little risk to you.

51

Example:

You have 7♠-2♣ in the big blind. It is late in the tournament. You have $220,000. The blinds are $4,000-$8,000 with a $100 ante. Everyone folds to you in the small blind. The small blind has $20,000. The small blind calls. What should you do?

Why would the small blind just call? He has $4,000 in the pot, and only has $16,000 left.

You have the worst hand in poker, but it doesn't matter. You have over ten times the number of chips as your opponent. Move all-in.

Example:

You have 10♣-2♥. It is the middle of the tournament. The blinds are $400-$800. You have $31,000 and are in the small blind. Everyone folds to you. The big blind has $2,500. What should you do?

Move all-in. Put maximum pressure on the player in the big blind.

Tip: What Are Odds? Why Are Odds Important?

a) The pot odds are the ratio of the size of the pot to the size of the bet. For example, if the pot has $800 in it, and your opponent bets $400, the pot is $1,200. For you to call that bet, you have to put in $400.

Therefore, the ratio of the size of the pot is $1,200, to the size of the bet or $400. $1,200 to $400 is 3-1.

b) The pot odds are important since you want to make bets where the pot odds you are getting are better than the odds of you making your desired hand. (An odds chart is in the appendix).

52

In the above example, if you flopped a straight draw your odds are about 2.2-1 to make your desired hand by the river. Therefore, assuming you are going to the river, you are getting favorable pot odds and should call the bet.

c) Implied odds are based on how much you expect the pot to be at the end of the hand. It is often calculated to where you plan on folding if you miss on the next street, but you will continue to play if you make your desired hand.

The implied odds are important since there are times where the pot odds are not good enough to call a bet, but the implied odds change a fold to a call.

Using the above example, if your opponent had bet $1,000 into the $800 pot, your pot odds are $1,800 to $1,000 or 1.8 to 1. These odds are not favorable for a straight draw. However, if you and your opponent have deep stacks, and your straight is not obvious when you hit, you may be getting favorable implied odds to make the call.

That is, if you hit your straight on the turn, you might estimate that your $1,000 bet will end up in your winning a pot of $5,000 or more. That would mean you believe you are getting implied odds of 5 to 1.

Heads-up against Daniel Negreanu:
Big Slick

In November 2002, I entered my first World Poker Tour® event at Lucky Chances in Colma, California. The interesting fact about the town of Colma is that it's filled with dead people; it's reported that 90% of its residents are buried in the surrounding cemeteries. It's always a little eerie and bizarre to drive past headstones to enter a card room named Lucky Chances.

It was the early days of the WPT® so no one expected the huge crowd that descended upon that small casino on a Sunday morning. As I made my way to my assigned table, I spotted Phil Hellmuth being interviewed by the WPT announcer Shana Hiatt. And, there were poker pros all over the place. It was very cool.

By the time I sat down, the cards were in the air. As I settled in, seated immediately to my left was Daniel Negreanu, nicknamed "Kid Poker." His big smile signaled a champion who knew he was about to control the action. After all, Daniel's charismatic personality and winning style had won him fame and millions of dollars. Today, he is probably the most popular poker player in the world.

I viewed this as a prime learning opportunity. And Daniel did not disappoint. He craved action, and entered almost every hand. I sat back as Daniel scooped pot after pot. He was beating everyone at the table, except for an older gentleman.

This grey-haired fellow was unfamiliar to all. His style of play demonstrated that he was not experienced at poker. When he played a hand, he would limp and just call all the way to the river. Sometimes he'd win, but more times he'd lose. Surprisingly, the only player at the table he was beating consistently was Daniel.

Four times Daniel went to the flop heads-up against this player. The betting pattern was the same each time. The man would limp, Daniel would raise, and everyone would fold except this one guy. Daniel would bet every street, and the old guy would call every street. At showdown, the hands would flip over and the guy would beat Daniel with a monster.

The fifth time they were heads-up, Daniel just checked the river and asked, "Okay, what do you have this time? Another set?" Sure enough, this old man had Daniel's number, as he dutifully flipped over a set of 8's.

A few hands later, I was dealt 10♠-10♣. The grey-haired novice was under-the-gun and he limped into the pot. I just called, being in an early position. Daniel raised, and the old man and I called.

I was more than a bit nervous playing my first hand against Daniel. I had never played against a poker pro before. I don't know why, but I figured he must've had pocket Aces.

The flop came with three rags, all 8 and under. We both checked to Daniel, who bet almost the size of the pot. To my surprise, the older man folded. I had an over-pair, but I was intimidated. I wanted to fold, but I called.

The turn was another rag. I checked again, and Daniel instantly bet the turn. This was not good. Now, I knew for sure he had pocket Aces. If I called this bet, I'd have half my chips in the pot. What should I do?

I thought about it for a while. I decided to try to find another 10 on the river. I called.

The river was a Q♦.

I stared at that card, hoping it would somehow change. How could I possibly have tried to hit one of the two remaining 10's on the river? It's like a 25-1 shot. I realized that I'd lost half my chips on a poor decision.

Sadly, in a defeated tone, I said, "Check."

Daniel sighed softly. Paused. "Check."

Huh? Did I hear that correctly? Daniel checked his winning hand?

I'm stunned. I took too long to show my cards, so Daniel turned over his A-K. My 10's won.

Wow! I beat Daniel Negreanu.

I know it was just one hand, but it was the first time I played a hand against a poker pro. I felt alive. Sure, I got knocked out later in the event, but as I drove past those dead folks and headed home, all I could think of was that one hand of poker.

Pre-Flop Moves: When Your Stack Size Says to Move All-in

24. Move all-in pre-flop as the first raiser when your chip stack has declined to nine times or less than the big blind.

The best plans can sometimes backfire. Your chip stack is low, and in order to get back in the hunt you must make an all-in move. The time to move all-in is when your chip stack is nine times or less the big blind. And you want to make this all-in move as the first pre-flop raiser.

Why nine times the big blind instead of ten times the big blind?

At nine times the big blind you are getting slightly better odds on your play. For example, if your pre-flop raise is three times the big blind, and an opponent moves you all-in, you will be getting roughly 2.25 to 1.

At ten times the big blind, you are getting odds of 2 to 1 in the same scenario.

And the reason why you move all-in and don't just raise three times the big blind is because you want to make it less attractive for your opponent to call your bet. Plus, you also need to accumulate chips and doubling up at this stage is crucial if you expect to win.

What about eight times the big blind? Where you draw the line between moving all-in with nine times or eight times the big blind is a personal decision. Either one is a good choice.

Example:

You have 7♠-7♦. It is early in the tournament. The blinds are $150-$300. You have $2,400. Everyone folds to you in middle position. What should you do?

If you raise to $900, and a player calls your bet, you are at a disadvantage since you want to hit a set on the flop. If the player moves you all in pre-flop, the pot will be $3,750 and you'll have odds of 2.5 to 1 to call. You will have to call.

Therefore, it is better to move all-in since you only have eight times the big blind, and you need to accumulate chips. Move all-in. You will win the blinds, or more than double-up, or get eliminated from the tournament. Embrace the risk.

Tip: Moving All-In From Early Position

When your chip stack falls to nine times or less than the big blind, you need to take a stand before the big blind gets to you again. If you have gotten trash hands, and now are in an early position, you are in a more difficult position than before. With more players to act after you, it increases the chances that an opponent will find a big hand.

It doesn't really matter what your opponents may have, you must make an all-in move. Don't just think pocket pairs, two paints, or any Ace. Add in the suited connectors. Even if your hand is only better than Q-6 off-suit, you need to move all-in.

Pre-Flop Moves: When Your Stack Size Says to Move All-in After a Raise

25. Move all-in with your good hands when you have eight times or less than the initial raiser's bet.

You need to accumulate chips to win a poker tournament. When you get a good hand and need chips, look for an opportunity to put pressure on your opponent. A good hand is a medium pocket pair or higher, as well as an A-J suited or higher. This is an aggressive play that can build your stack or knock you out of a tournament.

Example:

You have 7♠-7♦. It is in the middle the tournament. The blinds are $200-$400. You have $10,500 in late position. A player with $20,000 raises to $1,400. What should you do?

There is $2,000 in the pot. You have less than eight times the initial raiser's bet. If you call, you will most likely lose more than 20% of your stack. If you re-raise you are committed to the pot. And if you move all-in the following will happen:

> a) Your opponent will fold and you will increase your stack by almost 20%
> b) Your opponent will call and you will either get knocked out or more than double your stack size.

Calling is the play most players make. This is not a winning play. Folding is better than calling. Moving all-in is the best option. You need to take risks. You need to gamble.

Pre-Flop Moves: When to Move All-in in the big blind

26. Moving all-in when you are in the big blind and there are multiple callers.

In the middle or late stages of a tournament, there are situations when multiple players limp into the pot. With so many callers, it gives the player in the big blind an opportunity to steal a big pot.

The player who is most likely to be slowplaying a monster is the first limper. A common play is to limp under-the-gun with pocket Aces. Usually, if you get past this first player, the other opponents will fold.

Example:

You have J♣-8♣ in the big blind. It is the middle stages of the tournament. You have $6,000, and the blinds are $150-$300. A middle position player, with $10,000, limps for $300, as well as two other players and the small blind. There is $1,650 in the pot. What should you do?

It appears to be a good opportunity to increase your stack over 20%. If you move all-in for $6,000, you should take down the pot.

You move all-in. The first player immediately calls. Everyone else mucks. He shows A♦-A♥. Bummer.

The flop comes J♦-4♥-2♥. The turn is a 9♠. And, the river is an 8♦. You get lucky and make two pair. That's poker, baby! You gotta get lucky to win.

Pre-Flop Moves: Taking a Risk with Premium Pairs in Position

27. In the middle and late stages of a tournament, call with pocket Aces or Kings against a player you think has a premium hand and who has a deep stack.

Pocket Aces and pocket Kings don't come along very often in a tournament. When you get them, you want to figure out how to play them to maximize your chip gain. If you have a medium-sized stack and your opponent has the same or more chips than you, this move can be very lucrative when you trap your opponent.

The situation is best if you are heads-up against the raiser, he is aggressive on the flop, and you have position. In addition, if the hand goes to a showdown, your more observant opponents will be cautious the next time you call a raise.

Example:

You have A♥-A♣ on the button. It is the later stages of the tournament. The blinds are $1,500-$3,000. You have $32,000. The player under-the-gun, with $44,000, raises to $9,000. You believe this player has a premium hand. What should you do?

While an all-in move will most likely increase your stack to $45,500, a call could provide a bigger win.

You should also take your table image into account. If you have been aggressive, and all-in move may not be as feared and you'll be called. If you have been passive, an all-in move is more threatening.

Call the raise. When your opponent bets the flop, you can move all-in.

Pre-Flop Moves: Taking a Risk with Small or Medium Pocket Pairs

28. In the middle to late stages of a tournament, look to call a raise or even call a re-raise with a small or medium pocket pair.

It is important to differentiate between hands that a) can win a big pot or get you into trouble versus b) hands that are just trouble.

The hands that can win you a big pot or get you into trouble are small to medium pocket pairs.

The hands that are just trouble are "Borderline or Trouble Hands" that Doyle Brunson outlined in his famous book *Super System*. These are hands such as K-J, Q-J, K-10, Q-10, all offsuit, where even if you hit your top pair, you may be way behind.

Example:

You have K♠-J♣. It is the middle of the tournament. You have $7,200. The blinds are $300-$600. The player under-the-gun, with $12,000, raises to $1,500. You are in middle position and you call. The player on the button, with $18,000, re-raises to $4,000. Everyone folds to you. What should you do?

Just fold your hand. The player that re-raised has a premium hand or A-K. Even if you hit your Jack on the flop, what will you do when your opponent bets the flop? Don't get involved with this trouble hand.

Example:

You have 6♥-6♦. It is in the middle of the tournament. You have $12,000. The blinds are $300-$600. The player under-the-gun, with $15,000, raises the big blind to $1,800. You are on the button. You decide to call, risking more than 10% of your stack.

The big blind re-raises to $3,600. The initial raiser calls. What should you do?

The pot is $9,300. The button raise is only two times the first raise. This could mean he has pocket Aces. It is going to cost you another $1,800, so the pot odds are only a little over 5 to 1. However, the implied are odds are too good to fold. You call.

Did you even consider moving all-in? You'll either be isolated against the big blind, or get both opponents to fold. It depends on your read of the big blind and the two-times re-raiser.

Pre-Flop Moves:
How to Counter the Gap Concept

29. Counter the Gap Concept with a re-raise.

You don't want to get in the habit of being a limper. Players like to see flops cheap when they have hands like suited connectors, small pairs, middle pairs, and those trouble hands like K-J and Q-J. While you want to vary your play, always think raise first. And if you are past the middle rounds, don't even think of calling. If your hand is good enough to play, it's good enough to raise.

In *Tournament Poker for Advanced Players*, David Sklansky introduces the Gap Concept. The concept states that you need a better hand to play against someone who has already raised in front of you. The rationale is that players want to avoid situations where someone has already shown strength, unless they know they have a really strong hand. This is the thinking of a player who wants to survive a tournament. But if you play to survive, you will surely die.

Don't look to preserve your chips, look to accumulate chips. Use the gap concept to your advantage. If you notice players behind you folding too often to pre-flop raises, you should widen your range of starting hands.

In addition, if you notice a player in front of you raising too often, realize that this player may be using the gap concept to his advantage and probably doesn't need a strong hand to enter the pot first with a raise. Look to re-raise this player with calling hands. Make him fear your hand.

Example:

You have J♦-10♦. It is the middle of the tournament. You have $34,000. The blinds are $1,000-$2,000. Everyone folds to the player to your left, who has $58,000. He raises the pot to $5,000. You are on the cut-off. What should you do?

The instinct is to see a flop cheap with J♦-10♦. With a raise in front of you, you'll have to call a raise. The raise was a small one, so it might be worth it.

What do you know about your opponent? Is he strong or weak? Is he trying to steal the blinds from a late position?

From your observations of his betting patterns, you know this player tries to steal too often from this position. Therefore, re-raise and put pressure on your opponent. Let him think you have a premium hand that is better than his hand. If he folds, you will increase your stack to $42,000. It is a risky play, but one that can pay off.

Pre-Flop Moves: Why Tight is Right

30. When to raise, raise & raise again.

There are opportunities starting from the middle of the tournament to accumulate chips by simply raising without big hands. One reason is that many players want to survive and play it safe. Another reason is that after a long while, players who know that winning poker is aggressive poker, revert back to their comfort zones of playing a smart, cautious style.

When you notice you have fallen into the trap of playing it safe for a long while, you have an opportunity to raise and steal pots. When you notice that your opponents have fallen back into this style, you have an opportunity to raise and steal pots. You need to accumulate chips, and you can't do that by folding.

Remember that tight, safe play gives you the right to raise and accumulate chips:

1. Have you tightened up your play? If so, raise and accumulate chips.
2. Has the table tightened up their play? You'll notice that most hands are won without ever seeing the flop. If so, raise and accumulate chips.

Pre-Flop Moves: Don't Rush,
It's Okay to be Late

31. Don't show up at the start of the event; that way you won't face players who are calling with any two cards.

You've seen this on TV. It's a major event at the WSOP, and the announcers point out that the game has started yet Phil Hellmuth is missing again. The camera zooms in on Phil's empty chair. Every few minutes, the camera scans back to Phil's table revealing he is still missing. When Phil finally shows up to take his seat, the announcers poke fun.

Why is Phil late?

There could be many reasons, but one reason for you to be late is that during the early rounds players have so many chips in comparison to the blinds, they'll take a risk with almost any two cards.

Example:

You have Q♣-Q♦ in late position. It is the third hand of the event. You have $2,500. The blinds are $10-$25. Three players limp into the pot. You raise to $150. One player calls. The pot is $385.

The flop is 7♣-7♥-6♥. Your opponent checks his hand. You bet $350. Your opponent raises you to $700. You have $2,000 left. The pot is $1,435. What should you do?

Does he have a 7 in his hand? Or does he a heart draw? Or perhaps he has an over-pair?

Assuming you don't know anything about your opponent, you are in a difficult situation. A call will leave you with $1,300 and a fold will leave you with $2,000. Should you raise and test the strength of your opponent's hand?

(Note: While this is a tough hand to play in any stage of the event, it is more difficult in the early stages when players are more likely to hold any two cards given the implied odds.)

Before you sit down and start playing in your next tournament, skip the first round or two. You'll be surprised how few chips are lost. By the way, if everyone takes this advice, you need to show up on time and steal their blinds.

Pre-Flop Moves:
How to Vary Your Pre-flop Raises

32. Vary your pre-flop raises by using your position, table image, stack sizes, etc., to make sure you don't signal the strength of your hand.

One of the keys to winning tournaments is to be unpredictable. Observant opponents will start noticing the things you do out of habit. The easiest thing to notice is how much a player raises pre-flop given the strength of their starting hands.

Example:

    a) An A-x hand: "I want to risk a small amount, it's not a great hand. I'll put in a min-raise."

    b) A Premium hand. "I'm suppose to raise three or four times the big blind."

    c) Pocket Jacks. "Not freaking Jacks, again! I have to protect this lousy hand and raise six times the big blind."

    d) Pocket Aces after another player has raised. "I want to get more money in the pot without chasing away the raiser. I'll set a trap and just double his raise."

If you decide how much to raise based solely on the strength of your starting hand, you are making a mistake. You need to vary your game, and keep your opponents guessing. You win the most chips when your opponents make mistakes.

Therefore, before you raise consider your position, opponents, stack size, the players in the blind, etc. If you still end up getting into a habit of sizing your raises based solely on the strength of your hand, use the second hand of your watch. When you decide to raise, check the second hand of your watch. If the second hand is between 0-15, raise two times the big blind. If the second hand is between 16-30, raise three times the big blind, and so forth.

Or don't vary your raises at all; instead, always raise the same multiple of the big blind regardless of your cards. You won't have to worry about giving away information about the strength of your hand.

Pre-Flop Moves: Second-Hand Low

33. Second-hand low with pocket Aces or pocket Kings.

This is a move I learned from reading T.J. Cloutier's *Championship No-Limit & Pot-Limit Hold'em.* In second-hand low, someone before you raises the pot. You are near the raiser, most likely next to act, and decide to call with your pocket Aces or Kings. You are hoping that one of the many players behind you will find a hand, or make a play to win the pot. When he does re-raise, you can move all-in and put him to the test.

This is not a common play but it is a tricky one. The reasons why this move is rare are: a) players with pocket Aces or Kings want to minimize the number of opponents before the flop; b) it is unusual for three players to have strong hands on the same hand; c) a player wants to re-raise and put a squeeze play on.

Example:

You have A♠-A♥ in an early position. It is the middle of the tournament. You have $60,000. The blinds are $500-$1,000. The player under-the-gun, with $110,000, raises to $4,000. What do you do?

You decide to use the second-hand low move and just call.

Everyone folds to the small blind. He re-raises to $20,000. The player in the small blind moves all-in. You call. The small blind folds.

Your opponent turns over A♦-K♠. He doesn't improve and you more than double your chip stack.

Tip: Avoid Fancy Play Syndrome (FPS)

Poker players like to think they are smarter and better than their opponents. Players have big egos. They overrate their abilities and underestimate the power of their edges. As a result, they try to be tricky and play backwards.

For example, playing backwards or Fancy Play Syndrome, (FPS) means that instead of betting you check, or instead of checking you raise, or instead of folding you call. When you trick a player and win, it makes you feel smart but it often leads to a bad habit.

It's not bad to be tricky once in a while. But don't start to get too clever or you will lose hands you should win, and lose more chips in hands you shouldn't have even entered.

And, if you spot an FPS player, take advantage of their predictable style. They are predictable because they will do the opposite—calls will mean big hands, bets will mean draws or nothing at all, and checking is a sign of a slowplay.

Pre-Flop Moves: How to Represent Aces

34. Make the first and third raises pre-flop to represent pocket Aces.

This is a very powerful move against good players, and it's best used when you are heads-up. A third pre-flop raise means a player has a monster hand, and most likely it represents pocket Aces.

Example:

You have K♠-Q♣. It is the middle of the tournament. The blinds are $150-$300. The chip leader is in early position with $18,000. He raises to $1,000. Everyone folds to you on the cut-off. You are in second place and have $15,000. You know the chip leader is overly aggressive, and you don't want him to see the flop. You re-raise to $4,000. Everyone folds to the initial raiser. He re-raises you to $12,000. What should you do?

You have a good hand, but it's not going to stand up to a hand worthy of a third raise. Your aggressive opponent must have a big hand this time.

Fold. You have $11,000, which is a comfortable stack size compared to the blinds.

Your opponent mucks his hand. You ask him if he has Aces. He grabs his cards out of the muck and shows J♦-10♦.

Example:

You have Q♠-Q♣. You are at the final table. The blinds are $3,000-$6,000. The chip leader with $194,000 is in an early position. He raises to $18,000. Everyone folds to you on the cut-off position. You have $150,000, which puts you in second place. You know that the player who raised is tight and has had a great run of cards. Still, you figure you have the best hand. You re-raise to $50,000. (You should have just moved all-in.)

Everyone folds to the initial raiser. He moves all-in. What should you do?

You have the third best starting hand. Your opponent is more likely to have A-K than pocket Aces or pocket Kings. But if you call and you are wrong…you call. He shows A♠-A♣. You get knocked out.

Pre-Flop Moves:
The "No-Look" Blind Steal

35. The "No-Look" blind steal in late position.

Everyone goes card dead at a tournament. It's very frustrating and often leads to a repetitive stress condition known as "folding." Common side effects are a dwindling chip stack and a migraine headache.

Before your chip stack drops below fifteen times the big blind, you'll need to take a stand. It's time for the "no-look" blind steal from late position.

While this sounds silly, the fact is most players won't steal blinds when they look down and see a weak hand. Don't let your cards ruin a smart, position play. If everyone folds to you in late position, and you need chips, raise without looking at your cards.

Please understand that you must steal the blinds to win a tournament. So look to raise on the power position, the cut-off, the button and even the small blind. If your cards are going to dissuade you, don't look at them.

Just don't do it.

I was caught using my "no-look" blind steal at a Sunday tournament at the Oaks Card Club in Emeryville, California. It was late in the event, and I was card dead. The cards were so ugly, they frightened me away from every steal move. I told myself the next time I was on the button, if everyone folded to me, I was going to raise without looking at my cards.

Sure enough, next time around, everyone folded to me on the button. I raised four times the big blind. The small blind folded.

But, out of nowhere, the big blind called me out, and said, "You didn't look at your cards." I was taken aback, so I pretended to be confused.

The big blind restated loudly, "You didn't look at your cards!"

I was impressed. But I shook my head no and explained "I looked at 'em when I got 'em."

I could see he wasn't buying. He proudly called my raise.

The cards hit the table. The big blind checked, and I made a pot-sized bet.

My opponent paused and mumbled something, as he was clearly frustrated. He wouldn't let go, though, "You didn't look. I just know it."

Then, he just sat there and did nothing.

Now, I don't believe in calling over the tournament director in these situations since it may be construed as weakness. However, the other players were getting annoyed. I had to say something.

In a stern voice, I said to the player, "I'm not an idiot, of course I looked."

It got his attention. He mucked.

Now, when I use the "no-look" bluff, I always at least pretend to look at my cards. Make sure you do the same.

Pre-Flop Moves:
When Aces Look like A-K

36. Move all-in with pocket Aces when the amount of the raise makes it appear like you have A-K, and you are almost certain your opponent will call.

When you get dealt pocket Aces you want to maximize your win. Typically, if an opponent has raised and you know he has a premium starting hand, you will re-raise your opponent. He will call your bet, but fold if there is an over-card on the flop and his hand doesn't improve.

Instead, try to represent A-K by moving all-in. If your all-in move is an oversized bet, your opponent will interpret your hand as being A-K. He will call your bet, since he determines he is a favorite to double-up.

This is a play that works particularly well on-line.

Example:

You have Q♣-Q♦ in middle position. It is in the middle of the tournament. You have $36,000. The blinds are $500-$1,000. You raise in a middle position to $3,500. Everyone folds to the small blind. The small blind has $32,000. He re-raises you to $12,000. What should you do?

You call even though you think the re-raise may mean either pocket Aces or Kings.

The flop is K♠-10♦-2♥. Your opponent pushes all-in. You fold. He wins the pot of $25,500. Your opponent turns over A♠-A♣.

Example:

You have Q♣-Q♦ in middle position. It is in the middle of the tournament. You have $36,000. The blinds are $500-$1,000. You raise in a middle position to $3,500. Everyone folds to the small blind. The small blind has $32,000. He moves all-in. What should you do?

This over-bet smells of A-K. You are going to be a favorite against the A-K so you call. Your opponent turns over A♠-A♣. You get no help, and lose a big pot. Your opponent wins a pot of $65,500.

Pre-Flop Moves: The Stop-and-Go

37. Instead of pushing all-in when you need chips against a raiser, call the raise and move all-in on the flop when you act first.

The stop-and-go move is an alternative to pushing all-in pre-flop. It is a play that gives you an opportunity to win on the flop with the percentages on your side; that is, your opponent will miss his hand 68% of the time. The way the stop-and-go works is that you call an opponent's raise pre-flop, you are first to act on the flop and you have enough chips left to get an opponent to fold when you move all-in.

You can also use this move:
- against a player who has been stealing your blinds.
- by calling a flop and turn bet, and leading out with a bet on the river to look like you were slowplaying a monster.
- on the turn, where you check on the flop, call on the turn and bet on the river.

Example:

You have A♦-J♦. It is late in the tournament. The blinds are $5,000-$10,000. You are in the big blind with the short stack at $92,000. The first player, with $158,000, raises to $35,000. Everyone folds to you. What should you do?

You have a good hand, and need to accumulate chips. If you call, you are pot committed anyway. So, you push all-in knowing your opponent will call your bet.

Your opponent turns over K♠-Q♠.

The flop is 10♦-4♣-2♥. The turn is a K♣. And the river is a 4♥. You are knocked out of the tournament.

Example: Same situation with the stop-and-go move.

You have A♦-J♦. It is late in the tournament. The blinds are $5,000-$10,000. You are in the big blind with the short stack at $92,000. The first player, with $158,000, raises to $35,000. Everyone folds to you. What should you do?

Call with the plan of moving all-in regardless of what comes on the flop.

The flop is 10♦-4♣-2♥. What should you do?

The flop missed you. It doesn't matter. Follow through with your plan and move all-in with $62,000. Your opponent folds.

Pre-flop Moves: The Delayed Bluff Steal From Under-the-Gun

38. Call under-the-gun as a delayed bluff steal.

A tricky move is to limp under-the-gun with pocket Aces. The objective of this move is to get one of the other players to raise, so the player under-the-gun can surprise them with a re-raise. (A few players will make the mistake of limping with A-K under-the-gun, and then re-raise a player when they get raised. There is a big difference between pocket Aces and A-K.)

When you are under-the-gun, you can replicate this appearance of pocket Aces.

Example:

You have Q♣-10♣. It is the middle of the tournament. You are under-the-gun with $18,000. The blinds are $500-$1,000. What should you do?

You should fold, as you are in a weak position with a drawing hand. You can raise, and hope not to get re-raised. Of course, you are risking more chips with a raise. You can call, but won't that look weak to your opponents?

In this move, after you look at your cards, you need to pause longer than you normally would. This delay shouldn't be obvious, but just long enough that your opponents think that you are thinking about how to play your pocket Aces from under-the-gun.

Your opponents will be leery of your hand. And you'll usually find yourself against just one or both of the blinds. No matter what cards appear on the flop, bet out.

Pre-Flop Moves: How to Spot a Bluffer

39. Spot a bluffer and re-raise.

Sometimes players will say something which signals they are bluffing. Here are a few examples and how to bluff out the obvious bluffer:

1. You are thinking about raising pre-flop in the small blind. The player in the big blind says, "If you raise, I may move all-in." What should you do?

He is bluffing. He is trying to scare you. Raise and he will fold. If he had a hand worthy of moving all-in, would he tip you off? Of course not.

2. A player on the cut-off asks the big blind how many chips he has left. The player proceeds to bet that amount. You are on the button. What should you do?

This player is bluffing. He is trying to intimidate the big blind that is low in chips. Raise the bluffer and he will fold. If the player wanted action, would he try to get the big blind to fold? Of course not.

3. A player raises pre-flop and you have a good but not great hand. What should you do?

Ask the player a question about something totally unrelated. If he responds with a long answer he is not bluffing. If he is short with his reply, he is probably weak. A bluffer doesn't want to give anything away with small talk. Act accordingly.

Book Recommendation:
The Books of Bluffs by Matt Lessinger

This is a book you will need to read more than once. It's that good. It will teach you when it is right to bluff and why. It will make you more aware of bluffing opportunities and how likely they are to succeed.

To be a winning poker player you must bluff. While most players know that to never bluff is a mistake, they only use a small set of bluffs in their arsenal. As a result, they are missing out on bluffs that will get their opponent to lay down a better hand.

Don't let this happen to your game. While *The Book of Bluffs* mostly uses examples from limit poker, there is so much good information on bluffing it will inevitably help your bluffs in a no-limit hold'em event.

Pre-Flop Moves: The Squeeze Play

40. The Squeeze Play.

This is a strong move and it can give your chip stack a significant boost. Here is how it works:

A player raises in an early position, and another player calls that raise. You are in a late position and need chips. However, your hand is weak. You re-raise, putting the squeeze on the raiser. The raiser now has to worry not just about your hand, but the action of the caller behind him. He folds. The caller now folds since you put in a re-raise, and his hand was only good enough for a call.

Here are some elements that are helpful for the squeeze play to work:
   a. The original raiser is aggressive.
   b. The caller is not someone who sets traps.
   c. You are perceived as a tight player who will only re-raise with a monster.
   d. Your re-raise doesn't put you all-in. An all-in re-raise is often perceived as a weaker play.

Dan Harrington made this move famous at the final table of the 2004 World Series of Poker.

Example from the WSOP:

You have 6♥-2♦. You are on the button with $2.3 million. It is the final table of the main event at the WSOP. The blinds are $40,000-$80,000. The player under-the-gun, with almost $4 million, raises to $225,000 with K♥-9♠. The next player, who has $8 million, calls with A♣-2♣. Everyone folds to you. What should you do?

Fold, right? There is $570,000 in the pot. You have a tight table image and you have enough chips so that you can leave some behind the line. You decide to execute the squeeze play. You re-raise to $1.2 million, leaving $1.1 million.

The player in the big blind finds A♠-Q♣. But with a raise and re-raise in front of him, he can't play this hand. He folds. The original raiser folds his K♥-9♠. And now the caller has to make a decision. Should he call? He reluctantly folds. You take down a big pot.

Tip: The Squeeze Play is Not Just a Pre-Flop Move

The Squeeze Play is also a move that can be used on other streets as well. Some of the requirements for a successful squeeze play are the following:
- You are playing against two opponents.
- The player who takes the lead by betting or raising is between you and the player who calls that bet.
- The player in the middle just calls the bettor or raiser.
- When you make a big raise or re-raise, your opponents believe it signals you have a monster. This can be because of the combination of your bet, your table image and the community cards.
- And, of course, neither one of your opponents has a monster hand.

Tip: Squeeze Back the Squeezer

If you notice an opponent who uses the squeeze play, you may get an opportunity to squeeze back. You will need to have a good-sized chip stack since you will be re-raising a re-raise and want to get him to fold. If your poker instincts are right, you will win a big stack. Of course, if he has a monster, you are going to be buried.

85

The Truth about Poker Tells

A tell is any type of behavior or action an opponent does that gives you a clue as to the strength of his hand. The player who has a tell is not aware he has this tell. And if you notice this behavior you will have an advantage, as it "tells" you if your opponent is strong or weak.

Tells are hard to find, and when you do find one, you have to make sure it is reliable.

When I started playing limit hold'em at the Oaks Card Room in Emeryville, California, I would remind myself to look for tells. However, once I sat down, I became too involved in the cards to notice unusual behavior of my opponents.

After a while, I became more comfortable playing the cards and started looking for tells. Unlike in the movie *Rounders*, poker players don't bring Oreo cookies to the table like Teddy KGB. Tells are tough to spot.

One day, I was playing in a $8-$16 limit hold'em game and noticed the player to my right would bet his chips in two different ways. Sometimes he would bet so his chips fell forward, and other times he would make his chips go slightly to the right. I tried to see if there was any connection between how he bet his chips and the strength of his hand.

It took a while, but there was a link. If the chips came forward, he was weak. If he bet his chips slightly off-center, he was strong.

I decided that regardless of my hand, I would enter every hand that my opponent entered. My objective was to be heads-up.

It worked. I would know when to raise him and when to fold. It was like going to an ATM machine, except I was using his bankcard.

After about an hour of beating up on this guy, he turned to me and said, "It's like you know what I have." I replied, "I'm just getting lucky."

So, tells do work. They are just tough to find.

In tournaments, I believe the best players to study are the ones seated next to you since you are going to be in the blinds against them. For example, in one tournament I noticed that the woman to my left placed her card protector in different locations after she looked at her cards. If she placed the protector on top of her cards, she was going to enter the pot. If she kept the protector off her cards, she would fold.

Whenever action got to me, I'd look at my hand and wait for a few seconds. She couldn't help herself and she'd always peek at her hand. I'd wait until she decided where to place her card protector. Thanks to this tell I avoided trouble and accumulated enough chips to get to the final table.

One time I almost passed out trying to give a "reverse" tell. I was playing at a no-limit cash game at Lucky Chances in Colma, California. It was their biggest no-limit cash game of the week, so the players knew all about poker tells.

I got dealt pocket 9's. The player to my right opened with a raise. I called. We were heads-up on the flop.

The flop was 9 high. My opponent checked. When he checked I knew he was setting a trap. I put him on a big pair. How can I get the rest of his money?

He had $800, and I had him covered. With the pot at only $80, I knew that he would interpret any sign of resistance on my part as a signal to slow down.

I moved all-in. A crazy bet. But, I used a common poker tell to my advantage. The tell is that if a player makes a big bet and holds his breath, he is bluffing. Since the flop had two cards of the same suit, I knew my opponent would put me on a flush draw, if I used this tell.

I took a long, deep breath and held it. My opponent turned to his left and stared right at me. I raised my head up slightly, so he could see my face. As the seconds passed, though, he hadn't made a decision, and my face was slowly turning red. He kept staring. I could sense my face was bright red. More time passed, and I figured I might pass out any moment.

"Call," he said.

I sucked in the air as I flipped over my pocket 9's. He showed pocket Kings, and got no help. As I scooped the chips, he glared at me. I looked away since I knew, he knew, that I reversed a tell to win a big pot. He left the game. (A few years later I watched him win $3 million on TV by finishing 3rd in the main event at the WSOP.)

And that's a warning: Players know other players are looking for tells, and they can use your knowledge against you. So be careful whom you're watching.

As for poker tells, here are some general guidelines:

- You must commit to looking for a tell, to be able to find a tell.
- Try to pick one player at the table that you'll end up playing the most against, and focus on his play. The most likely candidates are the players to your immediate left and/or right since you'll be heads up in the blinds against them.
- Players who do anything different from the way they usually act in other hands, are the players who are most likely to have a tell.
- Players who act strong are weak, and players who act weak are strong.
- Players who use their chips to bet aggressively are usually weak.

- Players who peek at their cards after a flop comes with three suited cards, do not have two cards of that suit.
- Players who talk a lot after making a bet, and have previously been quiet for a very long time are strong.
- Players who make a bet and then are motionless and hold their breath are usually bluffing.
- Players who bet too fast when a scare card hits, don't have the made hand that scare card provided.
- Players who jump out of their seat after they move all-in pre-flop and have not made a play for a long time, and then stay to hover at the table, are strong.
- Players who get up from the table after they move all-in, and then walk away from the table have a good but not a great hand.
- Players who make a pre-flop raise and then watch intently to see if their opponents will act, have pocket Aces.

If all else fails, bring a bag of Oreo cookies and offer a cookie to your opponent.

Book Recommendation: *Phil Hellmuth Presents Read'em and Reap by* Joe Navarro

This book is a winner. Joe Navarro is a former FBI counterintelligence officer whose job it was to use nonverbal behavior as clues to determine if someone was lying. He transfers this knowledge to the area of poker.

Read'em and Reap gives you clues as to what to look for in your opponent's behavior and how to interpret these nonverbal signals. Believe it or not, it often starts at the feet! Importantly, it will also help you learn how to conceal your own tells. Phil Hellmuth admits that Joe Navarro helped him in his game, and I believe he will help you as well.

Don't just read this book, but also study it. It works!

Tip: Exercises to Improve Your Hand-Reading Ability

Hand-reading is about trying to narrow down the range of hands an opponent is playing against you. Here are some exercises to help improve your hand-reading ability. You will lose your money in some of these exercises, so select lower limits, but not at blind levels where no one ever folds.

Play a low blind, limit poker cash game and raise every hand pre-flop. This will put you in a situation where the action and play revolves around you. You will feel the power of being in charge. It will also put you in the position of having to make difficult decisions.

Play in a small no-limit poker tournament, and raise pre-flop once out of every three hands. Again, you will see how players respond to you. You will learn to be creative and build your hand reading skills.

Watch a table of limit or no-limit poker for an hour and try to identify betting patterns and put players on hands. Think about how you would have played against players, or what you would have done. This is easier to do online.

Do some player mapping. The next time you play in a tournament, actually write down notes about your opponents, especially their betting patterns. See if they hold true, and if it helps you to play better. Again, this is easier to do online.

Flop Moves: Steal-Flops

41. Bet the Rainbow "Steal-Flop."

A steal-flop is one in which a player who bets at the flop can be expected to win it uncontested due to the nature of the flop. The strength of the hand is unimportant. However, the player wants to have few opponents.

A rainbow steal-flop is one where the cards are different suits and the flop presents little opportunity for any potential draws. In addition, the cards on the flop are not likely to make a player top pair since they are of lower ranks.

Example:

You have J♦-10♦. It is the middle of the tournament. You have $45,000, and are on the button. The blinds are $2,000-$4,000. A player in an early position limps into the hand. You call on the button. The button calls. There is $14,000 in the pot.

The flop comes 9♠-6♥-3♣. The first two players check. What should you do?

It's a rainbow flop. There are three different suits. The cards are not coordinated. And the top card is a nine. Your opponents checked indicating weakness. You should bet. Bet $9,000 and expect to win the pot.

In fact, even if you are the first to act you should bet at this rainbow flop. The first player who bets at the rainbow flop is most likely going to win the pot.

42. Bet the Picture Card-rag-rag "Steal-flop."

Another steal flop is when the flop has one picture card and two small cards, and without drawing potential.

Example:

You have J♦-10♦. It is the middle of the tournament. You have $45,000. The blinds are $2,000-$4,000. A player in early position calls. You call on the cut-off as does the button and the big blind. There is $18,000 in the pot.

The flop comes K♠-6♥-3♣. The first two players check. What should you do?

You have nothing, but this is a great flop to try to steal. You only have to get past the player on the button, so bet as a steal.

Bet $12,000 and if no one has top pair or better you will win the pot.

Note that this play is not recommended if the flop had an Ace instead of a King, since players will often limp into the pot with a weak Ace-x hand.

43. Bet at flops with pairs.

When a flop comes with a pair, players typically feel uneasy. If the pot is small, players don't want to try to bluff off chips in fear of running into trips. Use this fear to your advantage, and bet at flop with pairs.

The fewer the number of opponents and the less coordinated the flop, the more often your bet will take down the pot. Your position on a steal flop is irrelevant. Just bet.

If you get called on the flop, you will need to decide if it's worth betting the turn. Is the caller likely to have trips or is he hoping to take the pot away from you if you check the turn?

44. To re-steal from the bettor who always bets at flops with pairs, just call.

Flops with pairs frighten players since they may be far behind on the hand if someone has trips. Why get involved even if your opponent is trying to steal?

However, if there are few opponents on the flop, and your image of the bettor is one who would try to steal, you should call his bet. If he is trying to steal, you will find out based on his play on the turn. Most players find it difficult to fire a second bet if they get called on the flop when bluffing.

Example:

You have 6♠-6♣. It is late in the tournament. You have $122,000, and are in the big blind. The blinds are $3,000-$6,000. A middle position player, with $98,000, raises to $15,000. Everyone folds to you. You put in another $9,000 to call.

The flop is 7♦-7♣-4♠. You check. The pot is $33,000. Your opponent bets $15,000. What should you do?

Your opponent has you beat, so just fold, right?

What if you call this bet? What hand do you believe your opponent will put you on if you call his bet? Probably, he'll either be thinking you have an over-pair or a suited A-7.

You call for $15,000. You are now in a position to steal the pot by betting out on the turn. It's a pot with $63,000.

Example:

You have A♣-J♣. It is late in the tournament. You have $98,000, and are in a middle position. The blinds are $3,000-$6,000. You raise to $15,000. Only the big blind, with $122,000, calls your raise. The pot is $33,000.

The flop is 7♦-7♥-4♠. The big blind checks. You bet $15,000. Your opponent calls. What are you going to do on the turn?

This is a difficult situation. You've invested $30,000 in this hand, and you have $68,000 left. You may have bet too little on the flop, or your opponent may have an over-pair. Could he have called you with A-7, and gotten lucky on the flop?

45. Bet flops when all three cards are of the same suit and you are against two or less opponents.

When a flop comes with three cards to one suit, it is an opportunity to steal the pot if you are against few opponents. The reason this move works is that your opponents know they need a flush to win. They may not think you have the flush, but if they don't even have one card of the same suit as the three on board, they have to fold.

Here is a tell when three suited cards flop. The players who have two cards of that suit don't look at their hole cards, while the players who don't have two cards of that suit always peek at their hole cards.

The next time you see this flop type, don't check your hole cards. Instead, watch what your opponents do. What they do on the flop will dictate how to play your hand. If they peek, bet your hand or raise their bet. If they don't peek, get ready to fold.

Finally, if you are fortunate enough to have made a flush on the flop (which will happen about 1% of the time), look at your hole cards. Don't be too obvious about it. Just peek a tad slower than normal to make sure your opponents notice you. You will get action from your opponents.

46. With three cards below the playing zone, bet with two or less opponents.

The playing zone is defined as cards from 9 through to Ace. Tighter players narrow down their playing zone from 10 through Ace. When the flop has three cards not in the playing zone, it's a garbage flop. Garbage flops are a good opportunity to steal the pot with a bet.

Of course, not all opponents will fold since they can't believe you have any part of a board with three rag cards. As a result, if you get called on the flop, you need to assess the situation and decide whether to bet on the turn or slow down.

Example:

You have A♥-K♦. It is late in the tournament. You have $240,000. The blinds are $5,000-$10,000. You raise in middle position to $40,000. Only the big blind, with $350,000, calls. There is $85,000 in the pot.

The flop is 8♥-5♦-3♣. The big blind bets $65,000. What should you do?

What could the big blind have? A pocket pair? A-8 suited? Or are you being bluffed? If you call, you are committing half your stack.

Fold. In poker it is "the right of first bluff." Meaning the player who bluffs first, wins.

Tip: Know When to Bluff and Not to Bluff on Flops

Always be ready to bet at steal flops, especially when you have few opponents and no one has shown strength pre-flop. Small pots are easier to steal.

If you get a free play in the big blind, opponents are more likely to believe your flop bet with a garbage flop or a paired flop from cards 8 and under.

If you have more than three opponents, trying to steal with these flops are more dangerous. And if there is a lot of strength shown by your opponents with pre-flop raises, a steal will be less likely to work. Not only because of the strength of their cards, but the size of the pot.

Flop Moves: The Continuation Bet

47. The Continuation Bet.

The player who took the lead in betting pre-flop wants to continue to show he has a strong hand by continuing his lead and betting on the flop. Importantly, this continuing bet or continuation bet is made even though the flop did not improve this player's hand.

This is an essential move to add into your game. The size of your bet is important, as you want to make it big enough to either win the pot on the flop, or put your opponent in a position to get poor odds to call your bet. Usually the continuation bet is 50%-75% the size of the pot.

The probability that your bet will be called increases as the number of opponents who also stayed to see the flop increase and/or the number of potential draws appear on a flop.

Example:

You have A♠-Q♣. It is early in the tournament. You have $4,000. The blinds are $100-$200. In a middle position, you raise to $600. The big blind calls. The flop comes K♦-7♥-2♣. The big blind checks. What should you do?

You missed. It happens often. Fortunately, you are against just one opponent and it is a rainbow flop. This is a good time for a continuation bet. If your opponent hasn't made at least a pair of Kings, he will fold to almost any bet. There is $1,300 in the pot.

You bet $700. Your opponent folds.

Example:

You have A♠-Q♣. It is early in the tournament. You have $4,000. The blinds are $100-$200. In an early position, you raise to $600. You get five callers, including both blinds. There is $3,600 in the pot. The flop is 10♦-9♦-8♣. Both blinds check to you. What should you do?

You missed. This is a highly coordinated flop, which makes it very dangerous. And you have five opponents. This is not the time for a continuation bet. You have a straight draw but you may be drawing dead. A Jack may give someone a bigger straight or if it's the J♦, it may give an opponent a flush. Just check your hand.

Example:

You have A♠-Q♣. It is early in the tournament. You have $4,000. The blinds are $100-$200. In an early position, you raise to $600. Both blinds call. There is $1,800 in the pot. The flop comes 10♣-9♣-4♥. Both blinds check. What should you do?

Missed again.

When you have an Ace in your hand, and you get more than one caller, the one card you don't want to see on the flop is a 10. The 10 is a card that will get action from players since it plays in so many drawing hands.

When players call a raise they will often have high cards, drawing cards or pocket pairs. In this example, with your A♠-Q♣, your opponents may have K-J, J-10, 10-9, or 6-6. This means that you not only have to deal with a flush draw, but possibly players who have top pair and a straight draw.

Still, this is a good time for a continuation bet. The flop missed you, but with only two opponents it is worth trying to win the pot. Betting 50% of the pot means that you only have to win one time out of three to breakeven.

Bet $900 and see how your opponents respond.

Example:

You have K♠-Q♣. It is early in the tournament. You have $4,000. The blinds are $100-$200. In an early position, you raise to $600. Both blinds call. There is $1,800 in the pot. The flop comes A♣-10♦-4♦. Both blinds check. What should you do?

While you missed your hand, you do have an inside draw to the nut straight. However, the flop has the two dangerous flop cards, the Ace and the 10. If you get check-raised, you'll have to muck. This is not a good time for a continuation bet. Take the free card.

Flop Moves: How to Defend Against the Continuation Bet

48. Moves to defend against the Continuation Bet.

Let's say you called a raise with your hand, and when the flop hit, your opponent made a bet. What should you do?

The first rule to winning tournaments is to identify weaknesses in your opponents. You should be watching how your opponents play. And one of the key observations is to determine how the pre-flop raiser acts on the flop.

Does the player make continuation bets? How often? How much are these bets? How does he respond to a check-raise? When he gets called on the flop, does he fire a second barrel?

Observe your opponents, and work hard to identify their tendencies and when they are weak.

• *Folding*: The most obvious time to fold is when there are three or more opponents, and the player who had the lead pre-flop bets again on the flop. A player who makes a bet on the flop with many opponents is a player who has a strong hand. It is not a continuation bet, but a bet that shows he is still strong.

Example:

You have K♣-J♣ in the big blind. It is the middle of the tournament. The blinds are $500-$1,000. You have $24,000. A player in middle position, with $35,000, raises to $3,000. Three players call, including the small blind. You call. There are five players, and $15,000 in the pot.

The flop is A♠-J♦-5♦. Both you and the small blind check to the pre-flop raiser. He bets $10,000. Everyone folds to you. What should you do?

While you have second pair, and the pot is now $25,000, this is an easy fold. Even if another player had called, and the pot was bigger, you should still fold.

• *Calling*:

If you are not sure if your opponent is making a continuation bet or is still in the lead, here is one guideline:

If there are two or less players who see the flop, and the pre-flop raiser makes a 50-75% pot-sized bet, call the bet if you have a piece of the board. You want to give your opponent the opportunity to show weakness on the turn.

Example:

You have K♣-J♣ in the big blind. It is the middle of the tournament. The blinds are $500-$1,000. You have $44,000. A player in middle position, with $55,000, raises to $3,000. The button calls. You call. The pot is three handed, with $9,500 in the pot.

The flop is A♠-J♦-5♦. You check to the pre-flop raiser. He bets $5,000. The button folds. What should you do?

The pot is $14,500, and it will cost you $5,000 to call. That is almost 3-1 odds. But, the odds are not as important as the read you get from your opponent. Would he make this small of a bet if he has an Ace? Wouldn't he want to bet bigger in order to get his opponents off a potential flush draw?

Call the bet, and see what happens on the turn. If your opponent has nothing, will he fire a second barrel and bet the turn? Or will he simply give up his hand?

Of course, if you knew from prior observation that your opponent makes a 50% pot-sized bet every time he misses, the correct play is to check-raise on the flop.

101

• *Raising*:

If you are not sure if your opponent is making a continuation bet or is still in the lead, here is a second guideline:

If you are heads-up and the pre-flop raiser makes what looks like a continuation bet, you should raise when you have a piece of the board. Give your opponent an opportunity to fold.

Example:

You have K♣-J♣ in the big blind. It is the middle of the tournament. The blinds are $500-$1,000. You have $24,000. A player in middle position, with $35,000, raises to $3,000. Everyone folds to you. You call. The pot is heads-up, with $6,500 in the pot.

The flop is A♠-J♦-5♦. You check to the pre-flop raiser. He bets $3,500. What should you do?

The pot is $10,000, and it will cost you $4,000 to call. Did he bet half the pot because he wanted you to call, or because he was simply making a continuation bet?

A raise will find out if your opponent is strong or weak.

Tip: Why Continuation Bets Are Dangerous to Your Chip Stack

Players have embraced continuation bets since they've been told it's a smart move. The rationale is that once you have the lead pre-flop, bet on the flop and hope for the best. Unfortunately, this is a huge hole in their game.

The stronger poker players know what is going on with this move. A strong player doesn't play his cards on the flop, as much as he plays your cards. He knows from watching you play your tendency for continuation bets. That is, if you always make a small-sized continuation bet on the flop, a strong player views this as weakness, and he will call, raise or check-raise your bet. (Plus, there is always the possibility that he hit the flop.)

A stronger player may call your continuation bet on the flop, because he has noticed that when you don't have a hand you check the turn. And, when you check the turn, he will lead out on the river and get you to fold.

Of course, a small-sized bet may indicate strength and want action, however, the reality is that a big hand is rare. So, the stronger player has the odds on his side.

Another signal of a weak continuation bet is when the flop is coordinated indicating many potential draws. A player with the lead pre-flop will want to bet big to protect his hand, and not small to allow himself to be outdrawn on the turn.

The next time you take the lead pre-flop, don't just ask yourself if the flop hit your opponents. Look at the flop type, and ask yourself what you hope your continuation bet on the flop will represent. If it doesn't seem likely to work, check your hand. It may be save you chips or it may allow you to make a play on the turn to win the pot.

Tip: How to Counter these Smarter Players

Of course, there are counter moves to these smarter players who have noticed your predictable, betting patterns with continuation bets. Here are some counter moves:

If you actually did improve your hand on the flop and your opponent calls your bet thinking you missed, check the turn as a trap. When your opponent bets the river as a bluff, you can call or raise on the river to win the pot.

If this smart player has seen you check the turn after getting called on the flop when you made a continuation bet, you can bet the turn as a bluff.

If you don't make the continuation bet on the flop, your opponent may be confused since it broke your betting pattern. So don't make the continuation bet on the flop, but make it on the turn instead. This is the delayed continuation bet.

Poker is a complex game that requires you to think at different levels. You should be thinking about what your opponent's hand is, what he thinks your hand is, and what he thinks you think his hand is.

Flop Moves: The Probe Bet

49. Try a probe bet when you are hoping to win the pot with little risk.

The purpose of the probe bet is to determine if you have the best hand on the flop and you can take down the pot with little risk. You want your opponent to fold. A probe bet can come from the player who took the lead pre-flop but due to a scary-looking flop wants to see if his hand is still in the lead on the flop. Or a probe bet can come from a player who did not take the lead in the betting pre-flop and hits a pair on the flop.

The size of the bet is small since you don't want to take a big risk. In addition, you want to make this play against not more than two opponents.

Example:

You have A♠-10♣. It is early in the tournament. You have $4,000 in the big blind. The blinds are $100-$200. In an early position, a player raises to $600. Only you call. There is $1,300 in the pot. The flop comes A♣-Q♦-4♥. What should you do?

This is a good time for a probe bet. If your opponent doesn't have an Ace, it will be difficult for him to call your bet. You can make a small bet of $400.

You bet $400, and your opponent folds.

Example:

You have A♠-10♣. It is early in the tournament. You have $4,000 in the big blind. The blinds are $100-$200. In an early position, a player raises to $600. Only you call. There is $1,300 in the pot. The flop comes A♣-Q♦-4♥. What should you do?

You bet $400 as a probe bet.

Your opponent raises your bet to $1,700. This is not the response you wanted. However, your opponent may know the best defense against a probe bet is the big raise. You have a tough decision here and may have to fold. It depends on your read of your opponent. Is he raising because he has a better hand or because he is bluffing?

Flop Moves: The Blocking Bet

50. Make a blocking bet when you want to slow down your opponent.

A blocking bet is a bet designed to try to stop your opponent from making a bigger bet. In most cases, you are afraid that your opponent will make a bet so large that it will make it difficult for you to call, even though you have a hand that is playable. When you make a blocking bet you are the first to act.

Some of the situations where you should consider using a blocking bet are when:
- you are on a draw.
- you have second or third pair and are on a draw.
- you know your opponent has you beat.

If you add this move into your game, you must make the same-sized bet when you hit a big hand, like a set. The reason is that you don't want your opponents to think it's safe to raise your small bets.

More players are using this blocking bet. Sometimes they have a big hand, sometimes they have a small piece of the flop, and sometimes they are making a defensive bet. If you notice an opponent who makes these small-sized bets and never has a big hand, raise him big and get him to muck.

Overall, whenever your opponent makes a small-sized bet on the flop, ask yourself if the bet is one that is asking for action or one that is afraid of action.

Example:

You have J♥-10♥. It is the middle of the tournament. You have $55,000 and are in the big blind. The blinds are $1,000-$2,000. A player in middle position, with $44,000, raises to $6,000. You call. The pot is $13,000.

The flop is A♥-K♣-10♦. What should you do?

You have third pair, an inside straight draw and a backdoor flush draw. You don't want to call a big bet, so you decide to make a blocking bet of $4,000.

Of course, if your opponent views your bet as a blocking bet, he will raise and force you to fold.

Example:

You have K♣-J♣. It is the middle of the tournament. You have $55,000. The blinds are $1,000-$2,000. A player in middle position, with $24,000, raises to $6,000. A player in late position, with $38,000, calls. You call in the big blind. There are three players. The pot is $19,000.

The flop is A♣-7♣-4♦. What should you do?

One of your opponents may have an Ace. Since you act first, and want to see the turn cheap, you bet $6,000. If you get re-raised big, you will be forced to fold. However, if neither player has an Ace, you may take down the pot.

Example:

You have J♥-J♦. It is the middle of the tournament. You have $55,000. The blinds are $1,000-$2,000. In middle position you raise to $6,000. A player in late position, with $38,000, calls. The big blind with $44,000 calls. There are three players. The pot is $19,000.

The flop is A♣-7♣-4♦. The big blind bets out for $6,000. What should you do?

See the dilemma? Does he have an Ace or a flush draw? And what about the player behind you? If you call, he may raise. Given the situation, you should fold the hand.

You fold, and think to yourself, "Why does this always happen when I get pocket Jacks?"

Flop Moves: Floating

51. Identify opponents who tell you if they are strong or weak by their betting patterns. Get heads-up against these players by floating, and when they check their hand, a bet will win you the pot.

Floating is calling a bet from an opponent you believe is weak in order to take the pot away with a bet (bluff) on a later street. One way to find weak players is to identify their betting patterns. Weak players will size their flop bets to correspond to the strength of their hand.

For example, a weak player will make a pre-flop raise, and then bet a small percentage on the flop if he has a mediocre or weak hand. He feels he is obligated to make a continuation bet, and simply follows through with his plan. But if he gets called on the flop, he will give up and check on the turn.

If you have position on this player, you can call him with almost any hand. What he does on the flop and/or turn, will tell you how to play the hand. You are not playing your cards. You are playing his betting patterns.

Example:

You have x-x. It is the middle of the tournament. You have position on a player who you want to float since you know how he plays on the flop.

The flop is A♠-6♦-4♦. Your opponent bets 50% of the size of the pot. What should you do? You know your opponent will make a continuation bet, and will check the turn if he missed. You call his bet on the flop. When he checks the turn, you will take down the pot with a bet.

The flop is A♠-6♦-4♦. Your opponent bets 30% the size of the pot. This looks like a probe bet from this player. Raise the bet on the flop.

The flop is A♠-8♦-4♦. Your opponent bets the pot. What should you do? A bet the size of the pot means he has top pair. Fold.

If you are out of position, you can also float by either calling the bet and check-raising the turn or calling the turn and betting the river when your opponent checks the turn.

Tip: Are You Being Floated?

Do you ever get the feeling that whenever you get raise pre-flop, the same player is calling your bet in position? Perhaps this player has identified you as a predictable player. Perhaps this player is taking advantage of your inability to follow-up your continuation bets with a bet on the turn?

Don't let this opponent take advantage of your play. Be aggressive. Change your play and surprise him by checking the flop, or making an over-sized flop bet, or raising the turn, or moving all-in. Remember that a player who is floating does not need a playable hand. Be aggressive and put this opponent on notice.

Tip: Time to Float or Fold?

There are many benefits to floating. But there are dangers as well.

First, there are many ways to float. You can float when you have position. You can float when you are out of position. You can even float when there are limpers and you are in a blind position; that is, if your opponents check the flop, lead out with a bet on the turn.

Floating can be dangerous. You don't want to be predictable or opponents will play back at you. And if you don't have a good read on all your opponents, you may want to limit floating to times when you have a playable starting hand, and miss on the flop. When you miss, you can decide if it is time to float or a time to fold.

Tip: The Importance of Position in No-Limit Tournaments

Here are some reasons why having position is important both pre-flop and on the flop:

Pre-flop:
- If you are acting in the first three positions after the big blind you are at a disadvantage. It's important to play tighter upfront, as there are so many players who can find a stronger hand and raise you out of the hand.
- If you are acting from the button or the cut-off position, you know the action that took place in front of you, so you can make better decisions on what action is best.
- If you are in the small blind, you need to understand that you have the worst position as you will be forced to act first on every street.

Flop:
- If you are the pre-flop raiser, you want to have position on your opponents since your decisions will be easier once you know the action in front of you.
- If you flop a big hand, it is easier to build a bigger pot in position. If you check-call an opponent, he will be cautious on the turn as a check-call indicates a stronger hand than a simple call in position.
- In position, you have more options on how to get the most chips in the pot.

A Baby, a Bluff, Lindgren and Ivey

A few years ago, I was playing in a $1,500 no-limit hold'em event at the WSOP. I was fortunate enough to sit at the same table for hours. I was steadily accumulating chips with nice hands and some key flop moves.

After a while, it was clear to everyone at the table that the tightest player was on my left. He entered few pots, and he would only raise when he had a monster hand. Let's call him Jim.

Around four hours into the game, Jim's cell phone rang. He walked a few steps from the table to answer the call. As a new hand was being dealt, Jim leaped back and stuffed the phone back into his pocket.

A player had raised, and everyone folded to Jim. Jim pushes all-in. It was out of character, and the raiser was about to muck.

"Call. I have nothing," interrupted Jim.

"Well, then," replied the raiser. And he mucked.

As Jim scooped up the chips, he was staring at this guy. It was weird.

The next hand was dealt. By the time the action got to Jim, the same raiser had upped the pot again.

"All-in," Jim declared, glaring at his opponent.

Everyone at the table flinched. We didn't know if this was something personal now or what. It got tense for a moment, when Jim added, "I have to leave, my wife is going into labor."

"Really?" I asked.

Jim nodded. I believed him, although I'm not sure everyone else did given the high stakes involved.

Jim's opponent was a believer, but he realized that if he called and lost the hand, he'd be out. The raiser called and showed K♦-Q♦.

Jim revealed A♠-2♣. The board helped no one, and Jim's stack doubled in size. Of course, one very unhappy player left cursing his luck.

Now, I asked Jim, "Why are you playing? Why not just leave now?"

Jim shrugged, as his next hand was dealt. As soon as the cards hit Jim's hand, he declared, "I'm all-in!"

"Wait your turn, sir," the dealer cautioned.

On this hand, a player limped in front of Jim, and yeah, Jim moved all-in. The limper had pocket Queens and Jim turned up 5-2 offsuit. Of course, the poker gods knew how to play with our heads, because a 2 hit on the flop. We all knew that Jim would win again.

We were wrong. It didn't happen, and the Queens held up.

Even though Jim had more chips to play, he swiftly backed away from the table and left the scene. His chips would gradually be blinded off.

Play continued, and after taking down a big pot I had become the table chip leader. I was thinking that my big stack had put me in a good position to win the event, when two players moved from another table to join our game.

Carrying trays and trays filled with chips, it was poker pros Erick Lindgren and Phil Ivey. They filled in the two empty seats just on the other side of Jim's chip stack.

I was dumbfounded. Yes, I know, they're considered two of the top pros in the world, but how could they have amassed so many more chips than me? I'd been playing a strong game, and I'm a small stack compared to them.

Of course, everything changed at the table. Lindgren and Ivey were in perfect harmony. They muscled everyone out of pot after pot. It was impressive.

Finally, Jim's stack was gone, so I got to play the button against these two pros. Erick was in the small blind and Phil was in the big blind. I peeked at my cards and found A♠-Q♦. I raised three times the big blind.

Erick folded. Phil folded.

I laughed briefly, relieved that they had folded. Yet, my neighbor decided to comment, "That laugh means you were bluffing." Wrong.

The next time I'm on the button I looked down to find pocket 4's. Again, everyone folded to me. I raised three times the big blind. Erick called and Phil folded.

The flop was J♠-5♠-2♠. Erick checked, and I figured I'd win with my pot-sized bet. I bet, but Erick check-raised me.

That took me by surprise. I needed time to think about this move. Was he strong or weak or somewhere in between? I decided he was mediocre, but his mediocre had to be better than my third pair. I folded.

As soon as my cards hit the muck, I couldn't stop thinking that I had made a mistake. As the game continued I kept thinking about that hand. Rather than playing the new cards that were being dealt to me, I was playing a hand I had mucked an hour ago. Of course, since I wasn't focused, I got knocked out.

I flew back home, disappointed with my play. That night, I found a WPT event on the Travel Channel and Erick Lindgren was at the final table. It was down to five players, when I watched a very familiar hand.

Erick raised, and then called a re-raise from the big blind. The flop had three spades. Erick checked, and his opponent bet. Erick doesn't have a spade. In fact, he doesn't have any part of this flop.

It doesn't matter, Erick check-raises his opponent. No! It's the same move. I should have never folded!

Erick's opponent doesn't have a spade, either. The flop missed him entirely as well, but he moves all-in. Wow!

Erick's bluff failed, and he mucked.

One day, I need to pay Erick back for that bluff. And one day, the next time I'm check-raised on a three-card suited flop, I'm all-in.

Flop Moves: How to Play A-K
When You Miss

52. How to play A-K when you miss on the flop.

A-K is a drawing hand. This means that A-K needs to improve to be a made hand: a hand with at least one pair. You will only pair up on the flop about one-third of the time.

Sometimes you push all-in with A-K on the flop, and sometimes you don't.

Here are some guidelines to A-K moves when you miss your hand:

- A continuation bet is the usually the best move against up to two opponents.
- Against more than two opponents, be prepared to check and fold.
- If an opponent bets into you on the flop, fold unless you have the right pot odds to play a drawing hand.
- If you raised big enough pre-flop to be pot committed, follow-up with your play and move all-in.

Example:

You have A♥-K♥. It is the middle of the tournament. You have $10,000. The blinds are $400-$800. In a middle position, you raise to $2,400. Only the player on the cut-off calls. He has $18,000. It is heads-up. The pot is $6,000.

The flop is J♥-8♦-4♦. What should you do?

This is a typical situation in tournaments. You have $7,600, and a pot-sized bet would leave you with just $1,600. You can bet $3,000 and hope your opponent folds. If he calls, what are you going to do on the turn? If you move all-in, and your opponent

117

has you beat, you may be eliminated unless you get help on the turn and/or river.

Sine you are heads-up, you move all-in. Your opponent calls and shows pocket 9's. Not good news, but you have 6 outs or a 25% probability of making one pair. (Outs are the number of cards you need to complete your draw or to make a specific hand.) The turn is the 4♣. The river is the A♣. Nice.

Tip: Why Hitting A-K on the Flop May Be More Dangerous than Missing

You raise pre-flop with A-K and get one caller. The flop comes King high. You bet and get called or maybe you even get raised on the flop. What should you do?

This is what makes poker difficult. You need to consider the cards on the flop, the table image of your opponent, the chip stack of your opponent, his situation in the tournament, and more.

Also, what does your opponent think of your playing style? If he thinks you are a tight player, he may think he can get you to fold your one pair. If he thinks you are an aggressive player, he may think you are bluffing.

Sometimes even when you hit you're A-K on the flop, you may be facing tough choices.

Flop Moves: What Does a
Yellow Light Mean?

53. Slow down!

What should you do if you have a premium pair, the flop is not threatening, but when you bet on the flop your opponent calls?

What should you do if you flop top pair, the flop comes three to a straight or flush, and you can't improve your hand?

Slow down! Keep the pot small. You don't want to play a big pot in these situations. In the first scenario, if you bet the turn and get raised, you are going to have to make a difficult decision. Next time, you should just check the turn.

In the second scenario, if you bet the flop and get raised, you will have to fold. So check the flop and wait for the turn card. If a harmless card hits, bet the turn.

Example:

You have A♦-A♣. It is in the middle of the tournament. You have $8,000. The blinds are $200-$400. You raise from an early position to $1,200. The big blind calls. He has $12,000. There is $2,600 in the pot.

The flop is 9♥-6♠-3♣. Your opponent checks his hand. What should you do?

This looks like an easy win with a rainbow flop, no big cards, and no flush draws. You bet $2,000, expecting to take down the pot.

Your opponent calls. What? Before the turn card hits the table, you need to figure out what is going on in this situation. This is one time where you have to consider your opponent has a set.

The best advice: When he checks the turn, check back. You have only one pair. Try to keep the pot small.

Flop Moves: When to Lead Out

54. Even if you are in the worst position, lead out with a bet when you have a pair against two or less opponents.

You need to be aggressive when you are against two or less opponents. The reason is that if you hit a pair on the flop, the likelihood that your opponents have also hit a pair is reduced. If you check, and your opponents also check, you have missed an opportunity to win the pot.

This play will not work as often if you have three or more opponents in the hand, and if there are multiple draws on the flop. The reason is that with more opponents, it is less likely that everyone has missed. And with a flop with multiple draws, your opponents may decide to play their draws.

Example:

You have A♥-10♥. It is early in the tournament. You have $4,000. The blinds are $50-$100. In an early position, you call the blind. Another player, with $2,800, calls. The player on the button, with $6,500, raises to $400. The blinds fold. You call the raise, while the other caller folds. There is $1,050 in the pot.

The flop comes Q♦-10♣-4♥. You are heads up, and have second pair. If you check, your opponent may also check if he missed the flop and wants to see the turn cheap. And if he bets, you have to decide if you want to call with second pair.

Be aggressive against the pre-flop raiser. Use a probe bet. Bet $300.

Example:

You have 8♠-7♦ in the big blind. It is the middle of the tournament. The blinds are $400-$800. You have $28,000. A player limps under-the-gun, and another player in late position calls. Both players have slightly more chips than you. The player in the small blind folds. There is $2,800 in the pot.

The flop comes A♠-9♦-7♣. You flopped third pair. What should you do?

You can check, and avoid trouble. Or you can seize the opportunity and bet out. If no one has an Ace in their hand, it will be very difficult for one of your opponents to call your bet.

Even if you are called in these situations, you can improve on the turn. But, overall, it makes more sense to be aggressive and make a play for the pot. Use a probe bet. Bet $500.

Flop Moves: How to Play Draws

55. Here are some guidelines on how to play draws heads-up and in multi-way pots.

Draws are an opportunity to represent a strong hand. When you flop a flush draw you will have nine outs and make your flush 36% of the time if you play to the river. Straight draws have eight outs or a 32% probability. A made flush is easier to spot than a made straight; which often makes it harder to get paid-off.

A. Heads-Up
You have an opportunity to be more aggressive with draws. Heads-up and in position, you can raise as a semi-bluff. If you get called, your turn play depends on the turn card. If you sense trouble, you can check the turn and take a free card. Keeping the pot small and taking a free card is an acceptable option. If you think your opponent's hand did not improve, though, bet the turn.

If your opponent checks first, assume he is weak and bet the flop. If you get called, you have to decide your turn play based on your read of your opponent. If you think you are going to be check-raised on the flop, you should check.

If you are heads-up and out of position, before you bet on the flop realize that a bet on the flop is really committing you to also bet the turn. The reason is that if you miss the flush on the turn and check, your opponent is going to take the pot away with a bet on the turn.

If you check and sense your opponent is weak, check raise your opponent as a semi-bluff. If your read is right, he will fold. If not, you are going to have a difficult decision on the turn.

B. Multi-way Pots
When facing more than one opponent, you need to determine the strength of your draw since one of your opponents may be on the same draw. You don't want to lose a big pot by being too

aggressive with a mediocre or low-ranking flush card, or the low end of a straight. Second best hands are costly.

In multi-way pots, the number of opponents and your position plays an important role in your decisions. The fewer the opponents and the less strength shown by their betting/checking, the more aggressive you can be in the hand. If a player has a strong hand, aggressive play on the flop will not usually work. You can wait for the turn to decide how to play your draw.

With a draw, regardless of the number of opponents in a hand, there are times where moving all-in on the flop is the right play. While the move is a semi-bluff and you would prefer to win uncontested, even if you get called you will have outs to win a big pot.

Finally, since you know which starting hands are drawing ones, you should have a plan before the cards hit the flop on how to play the hand. This means you must get a sense of the cards your opponent will be playing, and play your hand accordingly.

Example:

You have J♦-10♦. It is the middle of the tournament. You have $33,000. The blinds are $800-$1,600. Everyone folds to you in middle position. You raise to $5,000. The cut-off, who has $44,000, calls. Everyone else folds. There is $12,400 in the pot.

Before the flop hits the table, try to put your opponent on a range of hands. Since you have a J and a 10, the first range of hands to consider are ones in the playing zone without a J or 10, and are not strong enough for a re-raise, as well as medium and small pocket pairs. It doesn't mean that your opponent doesn't have J or 10; it's just not the first cards to consider.

The flop is A♠-8♦-4♦. What should you do?

You have a flush draw, but your opponent may have an Ace in his hand. Since the flop is favorable, you don't want to check your hand. If you check, and your opponent bets the pot, you may not have the odds to call and a semi-bluff raise can be correct.

Instead, use a blocking bet to get your opponent to slow down, or get him to fold if he doesn't have top pair. If he calls, you can hit your flush on the turn. However, you should lean toward betting the turn with another blocking bet if you don't think the turn improved your opponent's hand.

If you think your opponent has an Ace with a mediocre kicker, you can even try a check-raise on the turn. Again, how you read your opponent's hand is key.

Example:

You have A♦-J♦. It is the middle of the tournament. You have $33,000. The blinds are $800-$1,600. The player in early position, with $44,000, limps into the pot. Everyone folds to you in late position. You raise to $6,400. The blinds fold, but the limper calls. There is $15,200 in the pot.

Before the flop hits the table, what hands do you put your opponent on? The most likely hands would be ones in the playing zone that don't include an A or J, are not strong enough to re-raise, as well as medium to small pocket pairs.

The flop is K♠-10♥-5♦. What should you do?

You have an inside straight draw, but that King and 10 present a problem. If you bet your hand, and your opponent raises, you'll be ill since you could have had a free card.

Even though you are only against one opponent, check. Take a free card.

Example:

You have A♦-J♦. It is the middle of the tournament. You have $33,000. The blinds are $800-$1,600. The player in early position, with $44,000, raises the pot to $5,000. Everyone folds to you in late position. You call. The blinds fold. There is $12,400 in the pot.

You put your opponent on hands like K-Q, or pocket 9's to pocket King's. Even though you have an Ace, a raise from an early position may indicate that your opponent has an Ace, like A-K, or A-Q. An Ace on the flop may not be good for you.

The flop is K♠-8♦-5♦. Your opponent bets $10,000. What should you do?

You have the nut flush draw. The pot is $22,400 and you have $28,000. You have 9 outs with the flush draw, and possibly 3 more outs with your Ace. With 12 outs, you are a slight underdog at 45%.

You can't just call the bet, since you will have so few chips left behind the line. You will either have to fold or move all-in.

An all-in bet makes the pot $50,400. Your opponent has $29,000 left.

Move all-in. You will win a big pot if your opponent folds and an even bigger pot if he calls and you hit one of your outs. May the poker gods be with you.

Flop Moves:
Playing Against the Drawing Hand

56. When you put your opponent on a flush draw, call on the flop so you can make a big bet on the turn if he misses.

Some players like to be super-aggressive with flush draws and don't mind moving all-in on the flop. They only have 9 outs, yet they are willing to take the risk. When they are called, they are getting the worst of it since they hope to be paid even money on a 2 to 1 shot.

Other players are more careful with their draws, and are willing to call to see only the turn card. They almost always are getting the wrong price. You can actually induce these cautious players to take the worst path possible by getting them to pay to see the turn card at 4 to 1, and then see the river card at only a 4-1 chance at improving.

If you check on the flop and the flush card appears on the turn, you have probably saved yourself chips.

Example:

You have K♠-Q♥. It is the middle of the tournament. The blinds are $300-$600. You have $32,000. You raise in middle position to $1,800. A player with $30,000, in the big blind, calls your bet. The pot is $3,900.

The flop is K♣-8♣-4♦. The big blind checks. You bet $2,800. The big blind raises to $8,000. What should you do?

You have seen your opponent make this play with a flush draw, so you decide he is making this aggressive move against you. You could push all-in or you could call.

If you call, it will cost you $5,200, and the pot will be $19,900. Now, on the turn, if the club doesn't come and your opponent checks, you can size your bet to give him unfavorable odds, and induce him to call.

Specifically, the odds against him improving on the river are 4 to 1. With $19,900 in the pot, a bet of $10,000 will be tempting to him. That is, for a $10,000 bet, he will be looking to win almost $30,000 if the club comes on the river. However, he will not be getting the right odds.

Of course, the safest play is to move all-in on the turn when he misses, so it ends any chance of being beat.

Flop Moves: When to Bet the Nuts

57. Bet when you make a set or a full house.

Sets are hands that are often misplayed. Most players check on the flop, hoping to trap their opponent. Unfortunately, this is a mistake. Big hands want to win big pots. And, there is nothing more important to winning no-limit tournament than accumulating those big pots.

If you bet the flop and your opponent folds, the reality is that you were not going to win a big pot anyway. You may have won a small pot, but that's thinking small. Think big.

If you miss a set the saying is "no set, no bet." If you hit a set, the saying should be "yes set, yes bet." The first reason to bet is because your opponent will not put you on this hand. The second reason to bet is to give your opponent an opportunity to lose all his chips to you. And the third reason to bet is that it will make it tougher for your opponents to play against you later in the tournament.

The potential for a big pot is even greater when your opponent has a deep stack. Don't check your set to players who have a big chip stack.

The next question is how much to bet. If your opponent shows weakness, bet an amount that you think will keep him in the hand. If your opponent shows strength, double his bet.

Example:

You have A♠-K♥ on the cut-off. It is in the middle of the tournament. You have $31,000. The blinds are $500-$1,000. Everyone folds to you. You raise to $3,000. The button with $40,000 calls. The blinds fold. The pot is $7,500.

The flop is A♦-7♥-4♣. You flop top pair and top kicker. You know your opponent is aggressive and will bet the flop. You check. Your opponent bets $4,000. What should you do?

Your opponent looks weak. Maybe he is trying to steal the pot, or maybe he has a weak kicker with his Ace. There is $12,500 in the pot. You have $28,000. You raise to $14,000, putting pressure on your opponent to fold. Instead of folding, your opponent moves all-in.

Wait! Most players would instantly call this all-in move, since they have top pair and top kicker. Don't make that mistake! Your opponent either has two pair or hit a set. Fold.

You fold, and before your opponent mucks, he flashes 7♠-7♣.

Example:

You have A♠-K♥ on the cut-off. It is in the middle of the tournament. You have $31,000. The blinds are $500-$1,000. Everyone folds to you. You raise to $3,000. The button with $40,000 calls. The blinds fold. The pot is $7,500.

The flop is A♦-7♣-4♣. You flop top pair and top kicker. You decide with a flush draw on the board to bet your hand. You bet $6,000. Your opponent raises you to $12,000. What should you do?

This is a problem. Is he betting that you are weak? Is he betting a flush draw? Or is he betting a bigger hand than you? If you call this raise, what card do you hope will hit on the turn? A King? Another Ace?

Your decision is ultimately based on your read of your opponent. Since you know this player never raises with flush draws you fold. Before your opponent mucks, he flashes 7♠-7♦.

Sometimes when you hit your set, you can win more money if there's a flush draw on the flop. With a flush draw, you can either be aggressive and bet like you have a flush draw or your opponent could get aggressive with his flush draw.

Example:

You have 5♣-5♦. It is early in the tournament. You have $2,000, in middle position. The blinds are $25-$50. A player in an early position, with $3,000, raises to $200. You call. Everyone else folds. The pot is $475.

The flop is A♠-7♣-5♠. Your opponent bets $400. What should you do?

Ask yourself, "What action should I take to get the most chips from my opponent?" Some players will just call. However, if another spade hits on the turn this may slow you down, since you'll fear your opponent has a flush.

A better move is to raise this bet, and make it $800. A minimal raise seems like you are testing the waters; that is, you have a good hand but are not sure how good it really is. Your opponent may put you on a weak Ace, or a flush draw. If he has a hand like A-K, he may make a big re-raise to get you to fold your "good" hand. In this situation, you are going to win a big pot.

Importantly, do not make the mistake of thinking an over-pair is the nuts.

Example:

You have 7♠-7♥ on the button. It is early in the tournament. You have $2,000. The blinds are $25-$50. A player in an early position, with $3,000, raises to $200. You call. Everyone else folds and you call. The blinds fold. The pot is $475.

The flop is 6♠-4♦-2♥. Your opponent bets $270. You call.

The turn is a 2♠. Your opponent bets $400. You call.

131

The river is a 2♣. Your opponent checks. You check.

Your opponent's hand is not that strong, but he has pocket 8's. You lose. (Note: If you think your opponent is weak, a better move would be to raise him on the flop or turn.)

Even when you hit a full house on the flop, checking is not a good play. Bet your hand, and try to build a pot.

Example:

You have Q♠-6♠. It is the middle of the tournament. You have $41,000 in a late position. The blinds are $1,000-$2,000. Everyone folds to you. You need chips, so you raise to $7,000. The cut-off and button both call your raise. There is $24,000 in the pot.

The flop is Q♣-6♥-6♣. You flopped the nuts. You check, as does your two opponents.

The turn is a 10♥. You check, as do your opponents.

The river is a 5♦. You want to win something, so you bet $8,000. Your opponents fold. Bummer.

Example:

You have Q♠-6♠. It is the middle of the tournament. You have $41,000 in a late position. The blinds are $1,000-$2,000. Everyone folds to you. You need chips, so you raise to $7,000. The cut-off and button both call your raise. There is $24,000 in the pot.

The flop is Q♣-6♥-6♣. You flopped the nuts. You decide to bet, but make it a small bet to make your opponents think you are weak. You bet $10,000. The player on the button is the only one who calls. There is $44,000 in the pot.

The turn is a 10♥. You have $24,000, and move all-in. If your opponent folds you won an extra $10,000 from the flop bet. If your opponent calls, you will most likely more than double up your chip stack.

Flop Moves:
How to Set a Trap with Top Pair

58. Set a Trap: When you are heads-up, in position and flop top pair with an Ace or King, check your hand.

Poker pros are looking to accumulate chips and like to trap. One move they favor is to check when they flop top pair and act last. While it is risky, the reward can be a bigger win. Of course, this is a play that should be limited to flops that are not coordinated since giving a free card could cost you the pot.

Example:

You have A♠-J♥. It is the middle of the tournament. You have $38,000. The blinds are $400-$800. A player in the middle position, with $45,000, raises to $4,000. You call on the cut-off. Everyone folds. It's heads-up. The pot is $9,200.

The flop is A♣-10♦-6♥. Your opponent checks his hand. What should you do?

Check as well. It is true that your opponent could have a straight draw, but why not take a chance to win a big pot?

In fact, your opponent's big pre-flop raise may indicate that he has a pocket pair that he was trying to protect. So, if he has pocket Jack's, your bet on the flop will get him to fold. However, the check may give him the green light to make a play for the pot.

The only caution is that you want to avoid making this play if the board is coordinated and has draws. For example, if the flop is A♣-10♦-9♦, your opponent could be working on a flush or a straight draw. Checking would give him a free card. You should bet your top pair to protect your hand.

Flop Moves: Why Slowplay?

59. Avoid slowplaying with big hands on the flop. Big hands want to win big pots.

Slowplaying is using deception when you have a monster hand by playing it passively rather than aggressively. You want your opponents to be active in the hand so you can win a bigger pot. The danger of slowplaying is that rather than winning the hand, you may allow your opponent to draw out on you, costing you the pot.

Even when you are tempted to slowplay, you should realize that the better play is to bet your big hands. The reason is that as soon as you show strength with a big bet on a later street, your opponent will realize he's beat and fold.

The other advantage of being aggressive is that it will be more difficult for your opponents to know when you are strong and when you are bluffing.

Therefore, when you flop a monster, don't try to be tricky. You have a big hand and you need to build a big pot. Bet, build, and think big.

A final note: Two pair is not a monster hand. Bet, raise or check-raise on the flop.

Example:

You have 10♠-7♣. It is early in the tournament. The blinds are $25-$50. You have $2,000, and are in the big blind. There are four callers, including the small bind. The pot is $200.

The flop is 9♦-8♦-6♥. The small blind checks his hand. What should you do?

You have the nuts, but there are both flush and straight draws. If you check your hand, you are asking to be beat on the turn. If

134

you bet the flop, you will get action from a player on a draw. An opponent may even move all-in with his draw.

If there are just callers and the turn is a rag, you can move all-in and shut out your opponents.

If you check the flop and call a bet, your opponents will only bet the turn if he completes his draw. If you move all-in, your opponent will probably fold. Slowplaying will actually cost you a bigger pot.

Example:

You have A♥-9♥ in the big blind. It is early in the tournament. The blinds are $25-$50. You have $2,000. There are four callers, including the small bind. The pot is $200.

The flop is J♥-10♥-2♥. The small blind checks his hand. What should you do?

You flopped the nuts and decide to slowplay. You check. One player bets $100, and you and one other player calls. The pot is now $500.

The turn is a 5♠. You check to the flop bettor. He bets $500, and you move all-in. He folds. You won $1,000, but you would have won more by betting the flop.

Flop Moves: Bluffing

60. There are pure bluffs and semi-bluffs. When you bluff you prefer to have your opponent fold his hand. Therefore, it is important that your opponent understands the strength of the hand that your bet represents and is willing to fold his hand.

Bluffing is an important part of winning poker. The objective of any bluff is to get your opponent with a better hand to fold.

There are pure bluffs where your bet is based on the situation and your read of your opponent, since there is little chance your hand will improve. And there are semi-bluffs where you have outs to improve your hand and you are betting to win two ways: either your opponent folds or you hit your desired hand.

A typical semi-bluff would be a check-raise on the flop with a flush draw. You are check-raising to represent a big hand and want your opponent to fold. However, if he calls your bet, you have outs on the turn to catch your flush and win the pot.

Bluffs that are effective are ones that clearly signal to your opponent that your hand is stronger than his hand. A bluff can be made on any street. And sometimes a bluff can be set up by calling a bet on one street, and raising on the following street.

When you float, you are bluffing. Again, the simplest float move is to call a raise on the flop in position, call the raisers continuation bet on the flop, and bet when your opponent checks the turn.

Of course, not many players like to make big lay-downs. So if your opponent has a big hand on the flop, a bluff is not going to work.

Example:

You have K♠-Q♠. It is the middle of the tournament. You have $44,000. The blinds are $500-$1,000. A player in middle position, with $60,000, raises to $3,000. You call on the button. The blinds fold. The pot is $7,500.

The flop is A♥-9♥-8♣. Your opponent bets $7,500. What should you do?

You can fold, of course. If you call, however, you could plan to bluff if a heart, Queen or 7 falls on the turn.

Example:

You have J♠-J♥. It is the middle of the tournament. You have $44,000. The blinds are $500-$1,000. In early position you raise to $4,500. An opponent in middle position, with $60,000, calls. Everyone else folds, so it is heads-up. The pot is $10,500.

The flop is A♥-K♦-2♣. You check. Your opponent bets $4,000. What should you do?

Is this a bet that wants action? It may be that he has a hand like K♠-Q♣, and is probing to see if you are slow playing an Ace.

If you want to bluff on this hand, you need to tell a story that is believable. One way is to check-raise on the flop and try to represent two pair. If you get called, you must bet again on the turn if you don't think the turn card has improved his hand.

61. Heads-up and in position, call on coordinated flops to set up a bluff on a later street.

A coordinated flop is one with flush and/or straight draws. These flops give you the opportunity to play the board against your opponent's hand. When you call on the flop, you plan to win with a bluff.

137

Example:

You have 2♥-2♣. It is in the middle of the tournament. You have $60,000. The blinds are $1,000-$2,000. A player in an early position, who has $75,000, raises to $6,000. You call. The blinds fold. The pot is $15,000.

The flop is 10♣-9♣-8♥. Your opponent bets $10,000. What should you do?

This is an easy fold, right? Wrong. This is a coordinated flop. What if you call this bet? What will your opponent think? What if a 7, J, Q or a club comes on the turn? With all those cards you can take the pot away with a bluff on the turn.

Example:

You have A♥-A♣. It is in the middle of the tournament. You have $60,000. The blinds are $1,000-$2,000. under-the-gun, you raise to $6,000. The player on the button, who has $75,000, calls your bet. The blinds fold. The pot is $15,000.

The flop is 10♣-9♣-8♥. You bet $10,000, and your opponent calls.

What should you do when a club comes on the turn? Or what if the turn card is a 7 or a 10? If you fold on the turn, at least you still have more than twenty times the big blind.

Flop Moves: When Opponents are Weak

62. When everyone checks, bet when you are the last to act.

When someone indicates weakness, you should show strength and bet. The most obvious tell for weakness is the "check." In hands with three or less opponents, if all your opponents check and you are last to act, bet.

Remember, you are not betting your hand, you are betting your opponents' hands.

Example:

You have A♠-10♠ on the button. It is the middle of the tournament. You have $36,000. The blinds are $400-$800. A middle position player, with $20,000, raises to $2,000. The cutoff, with $42,000, calls. You call. The blinds fold. There is $7,200 in the pot.

The flop is J♣-9♠-3♠. Both players check to you. What should you do?

You have nothing. There may be some draws out against you, but your opponents checked their hands. When they check, you bet. If you win this pot, you will increase your chip stack 20%. Bet $5,000.

63. When everyone checks, and you are next-to-last to act, bet

There is more risk in this move, since there is a player to act behind you. However, you want your opponents to react to your play. The reality is that most flops miss most hands.

Use this move when you have only two opponents.

Example:

You have A♠-10♠. It is the middle of the tournament. You have $36,000, and are on the cut-off. The blinds are $400-$800. A middle position player, with $20,000, raises to $2,400. You call. The player on the button, with $28,000, calls. The blinds fold. There is $8,400 in the pot.

The flop is J♣-9♠-3♠. The pre-flop raiser, checks. What should you do?

If you read the pre-flop raiser as strong, you check. But given this flop, his check looks weak. The player on the button may have top pair, but what if he has a middle or small pair? If you bet representing top pair, he will fold a smaller pair.

In no-limit hold'em tournaments, the first player to bet often wins. Seize the moment, and bet as if you are protecting a vulnerable pair of Jacks.

64. Check-raise those small-sized bets on the flop.

Unless you know your opponent will bet small on the flop when he has a big hand, assume weakness. A small bet is one-third or less the size of the pot. It usually indicates that your opponent is weak.

Example:

You have 8♦-7♦. It is in the middle of the tournament. The blinds are $400-$800. You have $17,000. A player in middle position, with $20,000, raises to $2,000. You are in the big blind and are the only caller. The pot is $4,400.

The flop is K♠-9♣-4♥. What should you do?

You check the flop. Your opponent bets $1,200. What should you do?

140

This is a rather small continuation bet from the pre-flop raiser. It is a bet that either wants action or is afraid of action. Big hands don't happen that often, so check-raise this weak bet.

Check-raise to $5,000. If he can't beat top pair, he will fold.

Flop Moves:
When Pre-Flop Steals Don't Work

65. If you improve on the flop, bet your hand. If you don't improve, you need to ask yourself some key questions.

Stealing the blinds is a well-known move by all poker players. If you get called when you try to steal, you can't just give up. If you improve your hand, you should bet the flop. If you don't improve your hand, do not make a knee-jerk continuation bet. Ask yourself these questions:

- What range of hands do you put your opponents on?
- Do you think the flop helped their hands?
- What are their betting patterns from the blinds? Do they fold or defend? And how do they play on the flop?
- Did you pick up any tells?
- If you make a bet on the flop, what hand are you representing?

If you are against one opponent you should lean toward making that bet, or you make a delayed continuation bet and check the flop, and bet on the turn.

If you are against two opponents, you should lean toward checking your hand. If your opponents show weakness by checking the turn, bet.

Tip: How to Identify Betting Patterns

The best way to beat your opponent is to determine when he is strong, mediocre or weak. If you know when your opponent is weak, you "almost" can't lose. ("Almost," since there are those things called bad beats.)

To determine the strength of your opponent, observe his betting patterns. Watch his play and notice how often he raises pre-flop, and from what position. Watch how he plays when he is in the blinds. Watch how he plays on the flop, and the sizes of his continuation bets, probe bets, etc. Watch how he plays his monster hands and how often he bluffs.

Overall, determine if any of your opponents have a predictable betting pattern that connects to their hand strength. If so, you need to use this information in making your decisions. And don't forget, your better opponents are going to be watching you in the same way.

Flop Moves: How to Play in the Blinds

66. Overall, players tend to play too passive in the blinds. When you are heads-up and in the big blind, if your opponent checks the flop, just bet.

This is a routine play. The player to your right is going to be the small blind, when you are the big blind. If this player is cautious, you'll get to see flops for free. It is surprising how often the small blind will simply call, even though all the other players have folded.

When you are heads-up if your opponent checks, just bet your hand. Take your opponent at his word that he's weak.

If he check raises you on the flop, you can fold. You can adjust your image of your opponent and/or realize that he actually hit his hand on the flop.

67. When you are the small blind and heads-up, be more cautious since you are out of position. You want to win a small uncontested pot, or lose your half bet.

When you need to accumulate chips to win, you should look to raise in the small blind when everyone folds to you. Broaden the range of hands you will raise in the small blind to hands that include one paint card and any pair. You don't always want to come in with a raise or your opponent will just move all-in pre-flop.

Vary your play from the small blind based on the hands you are dealt.

In a situation where you called pre-flop, if the flop misses your hand, you can check and fold if the big blind bets.

If the flop hits your hand, you need to decide if your opponent will bet his hand. If he is a passive player, lean toward betting.

If he is an aggressive player, look to check-raise. In either case, try to win the pot on the flop.

The key in these heads-up situations is to realize that being out of position is a hardship and not one in which you want to lose a big hand.

Flop Moves: Over-Sized Bets

68. Make an over-sized bet on the flop when you have a big draw or want to represent a draw when you have the nuts.

When you flop a draw you have an opportunity to play a hand aggressively against your opponents. When your opponent bets on the flop, you raise an amount that is significantly bigger than the size of the pot. Of course, you can also move all-in.

Since opponents know an over-sized bet could be a semi-bluff, you can make the same play when you have the nuts. All you need are two cards of the same suit on the flop.

Example:

You have 6♦-6♣. It is the middle of the tournament. You are in a late position with $64,000. The blinds are $1,000-$2,000. A tight player who has been getting a great run of hands, has $80,000, and raises under-the-gun to $6,000. Everyone folds to you. You call. The blinds fold. It is heads-up. The pot is $15,000.

The flop is J♠-8♠-6♥. Your opponent bets $12,000. What should you do?

You hit a set, which looks like the nuts. Your opponent probably has a premium pair.

Your objective is to win all his chips. With the flush draw on the board, you have an opportunity to look weak by moving all-in.

Move all-in for $58,000. If he has a premium pair and puts you on a draw, he will call your bet.

Flop Moves: Moving All-in

69. Move all-in on the flop when a pot-sized bet is about the same amount as your chip stack, and you believe you may have the best hand or can bluff out your opponent. This play is almost automatic when you are late in a tournament, need chips and are heads-up.

There are times in a tournament where your bet on the flop should be an all-in move, as you may have the best hand or you may be able to bluff out your opponent. The all-in move puts all the pressure on your opponent. It is risky, but there are times in a tournament where you must take chances to win.

Always remember: Don't bleed-out chips late in a tournament. Take action. It is better to give yourself a chance to win first place, than to play safe and try to cash out near the bottom.

Example:

You have A♥-J♣. It is late in the tournament. You have $90,000, and are one of the smallest stacks left in the event. The blinds are $4,000-$8,000. You are in middle position and raise to $24,000. Only the player on the button calls. He has $150,000. There is $60,000 in the pot. You have $66,000.

Before this flop is dealt, you should have a plan of action. If you make a pot-sized bet on the flop, you will have $6,000 left. You do not want to save a small amount of chips. If you make a bet, you must move all-in on the flop.

What is your move on the flop? You made a pre-flop raise in hopes of stealing the blinds. It didn't work. There is a two-thirds chance your opponent will miss the flop. Your opponent has $126,000 left. Will he be willing to risk half his stack on the flop?

Given the situation, it doesn't matter what flops, you must move all-in.

The flop is K♠-9♦-4♦. You missed. Doesn't matter. You are betting that your opponent missed and will fold. You move all-in for $66,000. This bet may even look to your opponent that you have A-K. He mucks and you have increased your stack significantly.

Example:

You have 4♦-4♣. It is late in the tournament. You have $210,000. The blinds are $5,000-$10,000. An early position player, with $120,000, raises to $40,000. Everyone folds to you in the big blind. You call for another $30,000. There is $85,000 in the pot. You have $170,000 left, and your opponent has $80,000 left.

The flop is 9♠-5♦-2♦. What should you do?

First, your call in the big blind is a questionable move as it was more than 10% of your chip stack. Second, your opponent will probably move all-in on the flop given the pot size. Third, since you made the call, you need to hit a set to improve your hand into a winner.

However, you didn't hit the set, so you check. Your opponent doesn't move all-in on the flop. He bets $40,000. What should you do?

Fold. Get away from the hand.

70. Try to get all your chips in on the flop when you have 15 or more outs.

When you flop a great hand, like a straight and flush draw, you will have 15 outs and be a 54% favorite. Play aggressive, and since you are the favorite it's best to try to get all-in on the flop.

Of course, there is one caution with this play. You may not have 15 outs (9 flush cards plus 6 cards to hit pairs to your overcards).

If your opponent has two pair or a set, you really only have 9 outs.

Even if you do have 15 outs, you are not a favorite if you just plan on looking at the next card. That is, the odds against improving on the next card is over 2 to 1.

And if you miss your hand on the turn, you may be tempted to continue and see the river card. Again, you are over 2-1 against improving.

A big draw with 15 or more outs is a hand you want to play aggressively and try to get all-in on the flop.

Flop Moves:
Spotting All-in Desperation Moves

71. An all-in move by your opponent on the flop is often a sign of weakness and not strength. If your opponent's all-in bet is an act of desperation, call with your good hands.

There is no countermove to an all-in bet. You are either going to call or fold. Assuming chip stack sizes are similar, you need to figure out if your opponent is bluffing, or semi-bluffing with a draw, or protecting top pair, or has the nuts. And even if you catch him bluffing, you can still take a big loss.

Example:

You have 10♠-10♥ in the big blind. It is in the middle of the tournament. The blinds are $300-$600. You have $19,000. Everyone folds to the cut-off who has $22,000. He raises to $2,000. Only you call. The pot is $4,300.

The flop is 8♣-4♠-2♦. You check. Your opponent moves all-in for $20,000.

Why so much? Is this an act of desperation? Or is this just a bad play? Often, this is a bad power play from an opponent who missed with A-K.

You call. Your opponent turns over A♦-K♥. He gets no help on the turn or river and you double-up.

Example:

You have 10♠-10♥ in the big blind. It is in the middle of the tournament. The blinds are $300-$600. You have $9,000. Everyone folds to the cut-off who has $6,000. He raises to $2,000. Only you call. The pot is $4,300.

The flop is 8♣-4♠-2♦. You check. Your opponent moves all-in for $4,000.

You call. Your opponent turns over A♦-K♥. The river is an A♣. Bummer.

Heads-up against Shannon Shorr:
Hitting a Set

One of the young guns in the game is Shannon Shorr. He has won over $1 million playing tournaments and writes a blog for the *Card Player* web site.

I entered a $1,500 No-Limit event at the World Series of Poker in 2006. At my starting table was Shannon, who I had never played against. He was the most aggressive player at the table, but was careful to pick his spots.

I probably looked like the second-most aggressive player at the table, not because I was playing aggressive poker like Shannon, but because I was getting a lot of good hands.

We were about three hours into the event when everyone folded to me in a middle position. I peeked at my cards and saw 10♠-10♥. I had $2,500. The blinds were $50-$100. I raised to $300. Everyone folded to Shannon who was in the big blind, and with about $3,500. He called.

The pot was $650. The flop was K♣-10♣-5♦. Given our seated positions at the table, Shannon was way over on the other side of the table. He was first to act and to my surprise he bet out. He bet $600.

There is $1,250 in the pot. I think about how I am going to try to double up my chip stack. In my recent online poker play, whenever I hit a set on the flop I doubled the bet of my opponent, and usually ended up winning a big pot.

I raised to $1,200. Almost instantly Shannon moved all-in. The thought "he's got a set of Kings" flashed in my mind. Of course I called his bet.

When Shannon turned over his cards, I couldn't make out what he had but neither card was a King. I flipped over my hand. Shannon got up and leaned over the table to see my hand. He groaned when he spotted my 10's.

Shannon had two clubs and simply overplayed his club flush draw. Still, he could hit a club and beat me. Shannon watched silently as a player stated to me, "Good hand." I didn't acknowledge his words, since premature acknowledgement is a sure way to jinx your hand.

Fortunately, Shannon didn't hit his flush and I doubled up.

Turn Moves:
The Delayed Continuation Bet

72. The Delayed Continuation Bet.

One move that is very effective is the delayed continuation bet. As the pre-flop raiser and as the last to act on the flop, your opponent expects you to make a continuation bet on the flop. When you don't bet on the flop, your opponent will often become suspicious about your play. When the turn card hits and your opponent checks, you bet and take down the pot.

Example:

You have A♠-J♠. It is the middle of the tournament. You have $9,000. The blinds are $200-$400. The player under-the-gun, with $6,000, calls for $400. You raise to $1,600 and only the limper calls. There is $3,800 in the pot.

The flop is K♦-9♥-5♣. The limper checks. You check behind him.

The turn card is a 5♥. The small blind checks. What should you do?

Bet. Your opponent has not shown any strength. And your delayed continuation bet will look like you flopped top pair or better.

Example:

You have K♠-Q♥. It is the middle of the tournament. You have $9,000. The blinds are $200-$400. Everyone folds to you in middle position. You raise to $1,500. Both blinds call your raise. The blinds have slightly more chips than you. The pot is $4,500.

The flop is A♣-6♦-2♦. Both blinds check. You check.

The turn is a 9♠. Both blinds check. You make a delayed continuation bet of $3,000. Your opponents fold.

Turn Moves: The Action-Inducing Bet

73. The Action-Inducing Bet.

An action-inducing bet is one where you make a small-sized bet in hopes of luring your opponent into thinking you are weak. A small bet typically looks weak on the turn, and an opponent may raise you big. When he does, you can re-raise or move all-in. Sometimes your opponent will wait until the river to bet or call your river bet to catch a bluff.

Example:

You have 10♦-9♦ in the big blind. It is the middle in the tournament. You have $32,000. The blinds are $1,000-$2,000. A player in late position, with $29,000, raises to $6,000. You call. The pot is $13,000.

The flop is K♦-7♦-2♣. You check. Your opponent checks.

The turn is the A♦. What should you do?

You have a flush, and want to induce action. You bet $4,000. Your opponent moves all-in. You call.

Your opponent shows K♠-K♥. The river doesn't help him and you double-up.

Note: The above example is a situation where both players had strong reasons to bet the flop. The player with pocket Kings slowplayed his hand on the flop, and then magnified his error by moving all-in with a flush on board.

Example:

You have K♦-Q♦. It is the middle of the tournament. You have $32,500. The blinds are $1,000-$2,000. A player in late position, with $29,500, raises to $6,500. You are in the big blind and are the only player to call the bet. The pot is $14,000.

The flop is A♥-Q♥-2♣. You check and your opponent bets $5,000. You call. You now have $21,000. Your opponent has $24,000. The pot is $24,000.

The turn is the K♠. You check and your opponent bets $8,000. What should you do?

You turned two pair. His bet looks like he's weak.

You move all-in. You opponent calls and shows J♣-10♣. You don't get help on the river.

Turn Moves: The Blocking Bet

74. The Blocking Bet.

On the turn, a small bet can also be a blocking bet. Like on the flop, the blocking bet is meant to slow down your opponent. On this street, a blocking bet can allow you to see the river card cheap. Sometimes, you can get lucky, and the blocking bet can win you the pot on the turn.

If you add this move into your game, you must make the same-sized bet when you hit a big hand like a set. The reason is that you don't want your opponents to raise your blocking bets and force you to fold.

Example:

You have A♥-J♥. It is the middle of the tournament. You have $25,000. The blinds are $500-$1,000. The player on the cut-off, with $30,000, raises to $3,000. You call in the big blind. The pot is $6,500.

The flop is K♥-7♠-6♥. You check your flush draw. Your opponent bets $4,000. You call. The pot is now $14,500.

The turn is the 5♦. You're now down to $18,000. You still have the flush draw, and you want to get favorable odds to see the river. You bet $4,000. If your opponent calls, you're betting $4,000 to win a pot of $22,500—which is more than the 4 to 1 odds to improve on the river.

Your opponent shakes his head and flashes you A♣-Q♣. He tosses his cards into the muck.

If the pre-flop raiser misses on the flop and has his continuation bet called, he has few options when his opponent leads out on the turn.

Example:

You have 9♥-8♥. It is the middle of the tournament. You have $25,000. The blinds are $500-$1,000. The player on the cut-off, with $30,000, raises to $3,000. You call in the big blind. The pot is $6,500.

The flop is A♥-7♠-6♣. You check your straight draw. Your opponent bets $4,000. You call. The pot is now $14,500.

The turn is a 4♠. However, what hand are you hoping to represent with a bet on the turn? This looks like a good time to check and hope your opponent does the same.

Turn Moves: Fire the Second Barrel

75. Don't be afraid to fire a second barrel if your opponent doesn't show strength and you don't think he has improved his hand.

When you're the pre-flop raiser against one opponent, and you get called when you bet the flop, don't stop betting if you think your opponent is still weak. If he doesn't improve on the turn, a big enough bet on the turn should get your opponent to fold.

How do you know if your opponent hasn't improved on the turn? You can never be sure, but cards that should slow you down are if a flush card or straight card comes on the turn. Also, the scare cards like an Ace or King could be problematic. And since players call with second pair on the flop, your opponent may have hit trips if the middle card pairs on the turn.

Example:

You have A♠-J♦. It is the middle of the tournament. You have $34,000. The blinds are $400-$800. A player in middle position, with $30,000, limps into the pot. You are on the cut-off and raise to $3,200. Only the limper calls. The pot is $7,600.

The flop is 10♠-5♦-2♦. Your opponent checks. You bet $5,000. Your opponent calls. The pot is $17,600. You have $25,800.

The turn is a 2♥. Your opponent checks. What should you do?

Your opponent probably has a flush draw or second pair. The pot is too big to check. Move all-in.

Tip: The Value Bet on the Turn

A value bet is when you believe you have the lead, and bet to get your opponent to call and increase the size of the pot. While you want a worse hand to call your bet, you also don't mind a fold if your hand is not that strong. Even when your opponent makes a bad call, he can suck out on you on the river.

Turn Moves: The Delayed Bluff

76. A delayed-bluff is betting the turn in position when your opponent's flop bet has been called and he checks the turn.

So many players use the continuation bet that it is worthwhile to identify the players who give up on the turn when their continuation bet is called on the flop. You want to have position on your opponent, and you want to wait until the turn to make your move. When you get the all-clear signal, the "check" from your opponent, bet the turn

Sometimes, you may actually improve your hand on the turn, making your bet a semi-bluff.

Of course, there is the risk that your opponent improves his hand, or your opponent has figured out your play and is waiting to check-raise your bluff on the turn. Again, knowing your opponent and his betting pattern are crucial. If your opponent can fire a second barrel on the turn, why did you call him pre-flop?

Example:

You have 6♥-5♥ on the button. It is the middle of the tournament. You have $30,000. The blinds are $300-$600. A player in middle position, with $20,000, raises the pot to $3,000. Since you've identified this player as one who gives up after his continuation bet is called on the flop, you call. The blinds fold. The pot is $6,900.

The flop is A♥-Q♦-2♦. Your opponent bets $3,500. You proceed with your plan and call. The pot is $13,900.

The turn is a 2♥. Your opponent checks. What should you do?

Put your plan into action. Bet $10,000.

Turn Moves:
Bet When Opponents are Weak

77. Be the first to bet the turn if your two opponents check the flop and/or when they check the turn and you are last to act.

When your opponents check, take them at their word that they are weak. If you are in last position and your opponents check the flop and the turn, you should bet. While it is unusual for players to check both streets, you should try to steal the pot with a bet.

If you are in any other position and your opponents check the flop, look to bet the turn if the card is lower than the rank of the second-highest flop card. The reason for this is that any card higher than the rank of the second-highest flop card will have a higher likelihood of improving an opponent's hand.

Example:

You have 2♥-2♦. It is the middle of the tournament. You have $15,000. The blinds are $400-$800. A middle position player limps into the hand. You are in the small blind and call. There is $2,400 in the pot, with three players.

The flop comes A♥-9♦-5♦. Everyone checks.

The turn is a 4♥. You are first to act. What should you do?

This turn card looks harmless. Also, if you bet here, it may look like you simply checked your Ace on the flop in hopes of setting a trap.

You bet.

The big blind folds. The limper asks, "Can you beat pocket 6's?" You stay silent, and he folds.

Turn Moves:
What to Do When the Aggressor Checks

78. When your opponent shows weakness on the turn with a check, lean toward betting.

Sometimes you do get lucky. On the flop, you may have called a bet because you have third pair or an inside straight draw. On the turn, you don't improve your hand and are ready to fold when your opponent checks. His check is often a green light for you to bet, and take down the pot.

Before you make that bet, you need to determine if the turn card improved his hand based on your read of his hand. Also, you should have a sense of his betting pattern in these situations. If he has checked the turn and folded to a bet in past hands, a bet is a safe play. If he has check-raised his opponents on the turn, you should check.

When you are making plays on the turn, the pots get bigger and the decisions need to be right.

Example:

You have J♦-10♦. It is the middle of the tournament. You have $18,000. The blinds are $400-$800. A player, with $20,000, raises in a middle position to $2,000. You call on the button. The blinds fold. The pot is $5,200.

The flop is A♥-J♣-4♣. Your opponent bets $3,500. You call with second pair. The pot is $12,200. You have $12,500. And you don't feel too comfortable with your hand.

The turn is a 7♦. Your opponent checks. What should you do?

Since this opponent gives up his continuation bets on the turn, you should move all-in.

Turn Moves: Scare Cards

79. Bet when a scare card appears on the turn to steal the pot.

A scare card is any card that is dealt on the turn that appears to give a player a strong hand; usually, it gives a player a stronger hand than the player who took the lead on the flop. Common scare cards are Aces, Kings, and the third card to a flush or straight draw.

An example is when you call your opponent's bet on the flop holding a flush draw. When an Ace hits on the turn, even though it doesn't make your flush, you lead out and bet on the turn.

Example:

You have J♥-10♥. It is the middle of the tournament. You have $23,000. The blinds are $400-$800. You raise to $2,800 in middle position. The big blind, with $19,000, is the only caller. There is $6,000 in the pot.

The flop is J♠-8♦-4♦. The big blind checks. You bet $6,000 wanting your opponent to fold. He calls. There is $18,000 in the pot. You have $14,200. Your opponent has $10,200.

The turn is A♠. Your opponent moves all-in. What should you do?

This is a tough spot. What range of hands did you put your opponent on when he called the flop? What cards did your opponent call your raise with? Does he have a bigger kicker with his Jack? Is he on a draw? Is he trying to steal the pot since he has invested so much?

If you call his bet and lose you will be in real bad shape. But if you call and win the hand, you will almost double up.

You can see why this is such a strong play. In fact, other cards that would worry you on the turn are any diamond, a Queen, or

165

even a 7. In fact, in this situation your opponent may have figured out there are 15 cards on the turn that he could use to bluff.

Example:

You have Q♠-J♠. It is the middle of the tournament. You have $22,000. The blinds are $400-$800. A player in middle position, with $24,000, raises to $2,000. You call on the button. The blinds fold. The pot is $5,200.

The flop is A♦-J♦-4♣. Your opponent bets $4,000. You call. There is $13,200 in the pot. You have $16,000.

The turn is an 8♦. Your opponent checks. What should you do?

This is an opportunity to bluff your opponent off his hand. It is another example of why having position is so important.

Your opponent has $18,000. Move all-in, and put maximum pressure on him. Unless he has a great read on your play, he will not jeopardize most of his chips on a call with a made flush on board.

Poker pros are always thinking about how they can take the hand away from their opponents. Turn the tables on them, and look for opportunities where you can take advantage of potential cards on the turn that can get them to fold.

Tip: Stack Sizes Are Key in Turn Bluffs

When you make a bluff bet on the turn you need to know your stack size and your opponent's stack size. Your stack size has to be big enough to create fear in the heart and mind of your opponent. Big stacks instill fear. Small stacks do not. The percentage your opponent has committed to the pot also enters in the decision.

If in the previous example, your opponent had $60,000, he would be inclined to call your all-in bet. Or if you only had $8,000 left, the pot odds will compel him to call your bluff.

Being aware of chip stack sizes is important on all streets. But to make a successful bluff on the turn you need enough chips to intimidate your opponent into folding.

Turn Moves: The Semi-Bluff Raise

80. Be aggressive when you hit a double-belly-buster on the turn, if your bet will get your opponent to fold.

A double-belly-buster is when you have a two-way inside straight. You may hit a double-belly-buster on the flop. Or, you may hit one on the turn. If you hit a belly buster on the turn, it will give you at least 8 outs. With one card to come and 8 outs, your odds against improving are 4.8 to 1.

Being aggressive on the turn, however, gives you two chances to win a big pot. Either your opponent will fold, or you can hit your hand on the river.

Example:

You have 10♦-8♦. It is the middle of the tournament. You have $42,000. The blinds are $1,000-$2,000. A player, with $60,000, raises in middle position to $4,000. You are the only caller in the big blind. The pot is $9,000.

The flop is K♣-7♥-6♥. Your opponent bets $5,000. You call, planning to take the pot away if another heart hits, or if you hit a straight with a 9. The pot is $19,000. You have $33,000. Your opponent has $51,000.

The turn is a 4♦. Your opponent bets $8,000. What should you do?

You have a double-belly-buster as any 5 or 9 will give you a straight.

There is $41,000 in the pot. If your opponent has a pair of Kings or one pair, it will be difficult for him to call a big bet. Moving all-in is risky, but it may get your opponent to fold.

Move all-in. Your opponent mucks.

Turn Moves: The Naked Ace Bluff

81. Use the Naked Ace Bluff move.

The naked Ace bluff is when you are holding the Ace that is the same suit as the three cards on the board, and you use this information to bet as if you have the nut flush. Since your opponents don't have the nut flush, they fold.

The key to this play is to make sure your betting pattern makes it clear to your opponents that you have the nut flush.

Example:

You have A♠-10♦. It is the middle of the tournament. You have $29,000. The blinds are $400-$800. You raise on the button to $2,400. Both blinds call your bet. The blinds both have $30,000. There are three players and $7,200 in the pot.

The flop is Q♠-7♠-2♠. The blinds check to you. You check since if you get check-raised, you will have to fold. At this point, you should also be thinking about the naked ace bluff.

The turn is 8♦. The small blind bets $4,000. The big blind folds. What should you do?

This is an opportunity to use the naked Ace bluff move. Move all-in. Even if your opponent has the King high flush he will have a difficult time calling your bet. He knows that if he calls and is wrong, he will be knocked out of the tournament.

Example:

You have A♠-10♦ in the big blind. It is the middle of the tournament. You have $29,000. The blinds are $400-$800. The player on the button, with $30,000, raises to $2,000. The small blind, with $30,000, calls. You call as well. There are three players and $6,000 in the pot.

The flop is Q♠-10♠-2♥. The small blind checks his hand. You check. The player on the button bets $6,000. The small blind folds. There is $12,000 in the pot.

You decide that the button has top pair and folding is the safe play. However, you may be able to take this pot away if the turn card is an Ace, King, Jack, Ten or any spade.

The turn is 8♠. That's the best card for the naked Ace bluff move. You can check, but instead you decide to move all-in. Even if you get called, you have outs. However, if you were your opponent with just top pair, would you call an all-in bet here?

Turn Moves: When to Move All-in

82. Move all-in on the turn to show strength and get your opponent to fold.

There are times when you need to take risks and put maximum pressure on your opponent. Ideally you want to bet, raise or move all-in to represent a strong hand. Even though it is a semi-bluff, your opponent will have a difficult decision unless he has a big hand.

Example:

You have K♠-J♥. It is late in the tournament. You have $295,000. The blinds are $5,000-$10,000. You raise to $30,000 in a late position. The button, with $330,000, calls. The blinds folds. The pot is $75,000.

The flop is A♥-J♣-4♥. You bet $40,000. The button calls. There is $155,000 in the pot. You have $225,000.

The turn is an 8♥. What should you do?

The turn card may have given your opponent a flush, right? Maybe. If he paired his Ace on the flop, notice that he can't have a flush.

If he doesn't have a flush, and you semi-bluff all-in, he will be forced to fold. If you were in your opponent's situation with A♦-Q♦, would you call an all-in move?

Move all-in for $225,000. Your opponent mucks.

Example:

You have 9♣-8♠ on the cut-off. It is the middle of the tournament. You have $35,000. The blinds are $250-$500. Everyone folds to you. You try to steal the blinds with a raise to

171

$2,000. But the button, with $29,000, calls. The blinds fold. The pot is $4,750.

The flop is J♠-8♦-2♥. You bet $3,000. Your opponent calls. The pot is now $10,750.

The turn is the 7♠. You check. Your opponent bets $7,000. What should you do?

Your opponent probably has top pair. If you check-raise, you hope to represent that you made a straight. It's a strong semi-bluff move.

Will your opponent call your bet? It is a risky play, but even if you get called you do have some outs.

Turn Moves:
What Does a Red Light Mean?

83. Stop! When you have a premium pair, and the board cards indicate that you are in trouble stop betting. Keep the pot small.

Don't misplay premium hands. While they may be the nuts pre-flop, that can change on the flop and/or the turn. Pocket Aces are just one pair. Coordinated flops will attract players to outdraw you. And it's a danger sign when players call your flop bet when the board is a rainbow flop with cards outside the playing zone.

Keep these pots small and check.

Example

You have A♥-A♦. It is late in the tournament. You have $295,000. The blinds are $5,000-$10,000. After four hours, you finally get dealt pocket Aces. This must be a sign that your luck is about to change. You raise to $30,000 in an early position. The button, with $330,000 calls. The blinds folds. The pot is $75,000.

The flop is 8♣-6♥-2♠. This looks like a safe flop. No draws to worry about on this flop. You figure your opponent will fold to almost any bet. You bet $45,000. Your opponent calls. There is $165,000 in the pot.

The turn is a 2♦. You have $225,000. What should you do?

What hand could your opponent have where he could afford to call your flop bet? Does he have an over-pair like pocket 10's? Or did he hit a set—like pocket 6's or 8's?

Do you bet or check? All you have is one pair. It looks like the winner, but is it? If you move all-in, you'll probably only be called by a player who has you beat.

Play it safe and just check. Try to keep this pot small.

173

Turn Moves: When You Get Raised

84. When you hold one pair and get raised on the turn, think fold.

As happy as players are in hitting top pair on the flop, they often become miserable when they get raised on the turn. That misery can turn into stubbornness as they call the raise and suffer a big loss in chips. A good fold is a good thing.

A player will usually not raise on the turn unless he can beat top pair. Obviously, some players will take advantage of this fact and raise on the turn as a semi-bluff, or possibly even a pure bluff. You need to observe during a tournament who can and can't make a big bluff on the turn.

Example:

You have A♥-Q♣. It is middle of the tournament. You are the chip leader with $141,000. The blinds are $1,000-$2,000. You raise in early position to $6,000. The button, who is in third place with $93,000, calls. The blinds fold. There is $15,000 in the pot.

The flop is Q♠-9♦-4♠. You bet $9,000. Your opponent calls. There is $33,000 in the pot. You have $126,000. Your opponent has $78,000.

The turn is a 8♦. You bet $25,000. Your opponent moves all-in. What should you do?

What hand does your opponent have to raise in this situation? Does he have J-10 suited, a set or maybe he is semi-bluffing with a pair and a flush draw?

It doesn't matter. Top pair, top kicker looks good on the flop, but against a raise on the turn it looks ugly. Fold.

You fold. Your opponent shows 9♠-8♠ for two pair.

Turn Moves:
When Folding is Clearly the Right Play

85. Fold when three or more opponents see the turn, and you don't have a big hand or the nut draw.

Don't fall in love with one pair when you get to the turn, especially when you have three or more opponents on the turn. The only reasons your opponents are still in the hand is because they either have you beat already, or they have big draws.

Example:

You have Q♠-Q♥. It is the first hand of the tournament, and everyone starts with $4,000. The blinds are $50-$100. Three players limp into the pot. You raise to $600 on the button. Only the limpers call. There is $2,550 in the pot.

The flop is 9♦-8♦-5♣. Everyone checks. You bet $1,800. Three players call. The pot is $9,750. This is not good.

The turn is a 10♣. The action is checked to you. What should you do?

The turn card didn't matter. You were done with this hand when three players called on the flop. Maybe two players could be on a straight and/or flush draw. But when three players call your bet, there are just too many ways you can lose.

The 10♣ on the turn did not help your situation, even though a Jack may give you the nuts. While you lost more than half your chips on this hand, you should check and hope to hit the Jack on the river—but not the Jack of diamonds.

Turn Moves: Picking Off Bluffs

86. Some pointers on how to pick off bluffs on the turn.

First, you need to know your opponent's betting patterns. How has he played the turn? Did he fire a second barrel without the goods? Or was he making turn bets given the value of his hand and the hands of his opponents? How large were his bets?

Second, it is often easier to pick off a bluff if you have position. You observed his behavior when you called his bet on the flop. When the turn card hits you can see how he reacts and how he sizes his bets. You can raise your opponent on the turn to put him to the test. Or you can call again to keep the pot smaller. If he doesn't have a big hand, your call will add pressure to his decision on how to play the river.

Third, you need to especially watch for semi-bluffs on the turn. Does your opponent's turn bet make sense given his prior action? If it is inconsistent, was he slowplaying or is he trying to intimidate you to fold?

Fourth, a potential tell is how fast your opponent bets the turn. If a scare card hits the turn, a player will naturally want to think about his next move. If he speeds up his bet when a scare card hits, it may be a sign that he is not strong and that scare card has not helped his hand. Of course, it does not mean that he is weak either. So if you call, you may still need to beat top pair.

Finally, picking off a bluff requires a great deal of experience. When you can pick off turn card bluffs and semi-bluffs, you are entering the highest skill levels of poker.

Heads-up against Layne Flack

I played against Layne at a $1,000 buy-in event a few years ago. He is an excellent player and actually a lot of fun to watch. He is one of the Poker pros that will call a raise with any two cards, because he knows he can outplay his opponent. In this event, he was building a nice-sized chip stack, playing big cards and small cards.

An interesting hand came up when a real tight player raised under-the-gun. Layne, from the middle position, called. The flop came 7♠-5♦-3♥.

The raiser seemed a little confused. He checked. Well, any time a player checked to Layne, he was going to bet. Layne made a pot-sized bet, and his opponent thought for a while, and reluctantly called.

As I am watching this, I had no clue what was going on. I knew Layne would try to steal the pot on the flop if the guy checked. But, this guy was acting strange.

The turn was a J♠. The pre-flop raiser checked again. Layne smiled this big, mischievous smile. Layne smiles a lot. He looked at his opponent, who wouldn't even look up from the table. Layne took a sip of his beer.

Layne bet half the size of the pot. Bam! His opponent moved all-in!

Finally, someone trapped Layne.

Wrong! Layne called.

His opponent, thinking he'd won, jumped up and proudly displayed A♦-A♣.

Layne revealed the nuts, 6♣-4♣. Amazing!

This guy who had been so happy one moment, got pissed. He snarled at Layne, and shouted at him, "You're an idiot!"

Layne just smiled and raked in the pot. He wasn't bothered by this outburst at all. His opponent stomped off.

About one hour later, Layne and I were at the same table again. There were only about six tables left. This time he was seated to my right, and in the small blind.

Everyone folded to Layne. He raised, no surprise. Layne had a good-sized chip stack at the time, but I had been running good and had a few more chips than him.

I decided to call with my J♠-10♥. It's better than a random hand, and I didn't want Layne to push me around in the blinds.

The flop was K♠-J♥-4♥. Layne made a pot-sized bet.

I figured Layne could have any two cards. The one card I dismissed out-of-hand was a King. Since I thought I was ahead, I moved all-in to end the action.

Layne called immediately! He turned over K♣-10♣.

Unreal. He had me. Amazing!

I pushed back in my chair ready to get up.

The turn was a 2♥. I turned around to leave, not even bothering to watch the river card hit the table.

The people around the tabled let out a groan.

A friend, watching the game, laughed and said to me, "You gotta flush."

Heck, I didn't even think I had a flush draw! I looked back to the table.

The river was a 6♥. Runner-runner flush. I had knocked Layne out of the tournament.

I sat down, as Layne got up. He started for the rail, and stopped halfway to turn and look back. He was still smiling, and he was still enjoying his drink. He took the bad beat in stride. The guy is a Pro.

River Moves: The Value Bet

87. Bet to increase the size of the pot when you think you have the better hand, unless your opponent will only call you when he has you beat.

Betting in poker is about getting a player with a better hand to fold or a player with a worse hand to call. A value bet on the river is meant to increase the size of the pot and to get your opponent to call with a worse hand.

However, it is not always right to bet on the end when you think you are ahead. For example, if you put your opponent on a missed draw and bet on the river you will find out one of two things: a) you are right, and he folds or b) you are wrong, and he calls with a better hand. Or worse yet, he raises your bet.

Instead, if you are to act first, and are not sure where your opponent is at in a hand, you can make a small bet. You can think of this bet as part value and part blocking bet.

Example:

You have A♥-J♥. It is the middle of the tournament. You have $45,000. The blinds are $500-$1,000. The player on the cut-off, with $50,000, raises to $3,000. You call in the big blind. The pot is $6,500.

The flop is A♠-7♠-6♦. You bet your top pair, with $4,000. Your opponent calls. The pot is now $14,500.

The turn is the 7♦. You're stack is at $38,000. You bet $8,000. Your opponent calls. There is $30,500 in the pot.

The river is a 10♥. What should you do?

You have $30,000. Your opponent has $35,000. If he had a better hand than you, wouldn't he have raised by now?

You can't safely make a value bet since you figure the only hands he will call with will be better than yours. If you check, and your opponent makes a big bet you will be forced into a difficult decision. Instead make a small bet.

You bet $10,000. Your opponent calls. He has A♣-J♦. It is a split pot.

Example:

You have A♥-K♥. It is the middle of the tournament. You have $45,000. The blinds are $500-$1,000. You raise in early position to $3,000. Only the player on the button, with $50,000, calls your bet. The pot is $7,500.

The flop is A♣-7♠-6♦. You bet $6,000. Your opponent calls. The pot is now $19,500.

The turn is the 7♦. You're stack is at $36,000. You bet $15,000. Your opponent calls. There is $49,500 in the pot.

The river is a 10♥. What should you do?

Your opponent has not shown any indication that his hand is better than top pair. You have the best kicker. If you check, your opponent will probably check behind you.

Is this a place for a value bet? How does the pot size and your chip stack influence your decision?

To get full value of your hand, move all-in.

You move all-in. Your opponent calls. He has A♠-Q♦. You double up.

In this example if you had position on your opponent, your decisions would have been easier. On the flop you could call his bet. On the turn, if he bets again you could call again. And if he checked the river, you could move all-in.

River Moves: The Blocking Bet

88. Make a blocking bet when you want to slow down your opponent on the river.

A blocking bet can also be used on the river to stop your opponent from:
- Bluffing, especially if a scare card appears on the river.
- Making a bet so big that you have a difficult decision to call or not.

Also, a small bet on the river can get your opponent to fold.

If your opponent knows you make these blocking bets, he may raise to force you to fold. Against this kind of an opponent, you are going to have to check and call his river bet.

Example:

You have A♠-9♠ in the big blind. It is the middle of the tournament. The blinds are $400-$800. You have $35,000. Everyone folds to the button. He has $40,000 and raises to $2,000. The player in the small blind folds. You call. There is $4,400 in the pot.

The flop is A♥-8♠-4♦. You check. Your opponent bets $2,000. You call. The pot is $8,400. You have $31,000. Your opponent has $36,000.

The turn is a 6♦. You check. Your opponent bets $5,000. You call. The pot is $18,400. You have $26,000. Your opponent has $31,000.

The river is a J♣. What should you do?

You don't want to call a big bet from your opponent. A blocking bet would keep the pot small and it is possible that the J♣ may slow him down.

You bet $4,000. Your opponent calls. He has A♣-10♣, and has you out-kicked.

River Moves: Getting Paid Off

89. Maximize your big hands with a bet that will induce your opponent to call.

When you know you have the best hand, you want to get paid off at full price. The challenge is deciding the size of your bet. Most players like to make small bets with the nuts on the river, thinking a smaller bet will make it easier for their opponent to call. Of course, their opponent expects a small bet with a big hand, and simply folds.

At times a big bet signals a bluff to a player since he expected a small bet. As a result, thinking that he is being bluffed that player is more likely to call the big bet.

Don't automatically mini-size your bets when you have the best hand or the nuts. And don't assume that your smaller bets are more likely to get called than your bigger bets.

Example:

You have 8♠-8♥. It is the middle of the tournament. You have $35,000. The blinds are $300-$600. You raise to $1,200 in a middle position. Your opponent, with $38,000, calls on the button. Everyone else folds. The pot is $3,300.

The flop is 8♦-4♦-3♦. You bet $2,000. Your opponent calls. The pot is $7,300. You have $31,800. Your opponent has $34,800.

The turn is an A♦. You check with four cards to a flush on the board. Your opponent bets $5,300. The pot is $12,600. You know you are beat, but the implied odds are excellent. That is, if you make your full house, you can win a very big pot. If not, you have to fold. You call. The pot is $17,900. You have $26,500 and your opponent has $29,500.

The river is a 3♣. What should you do?

You got lucky and made a full house. Your opponent has the flush, of course. How much should you bet?

If your opponent has the nut flush, he probably "knows" he is beat when you make a small bet. If he has the nut flush, though, he will call your bet. If he doesn't have a high diamond, he may fold to a small bet.

However, if you move all-in, your opponent will probably still call your bet with the nut flush, and he may even decide to call with any flush. An all-in move looks suspicious at the end when you have the nuts.

You move all-in. Your opponent calls. He has the Ace-high flush.

River Moves: Firing the Third Barrel

90. Firing a third barrel makes sense only if you are sure your opponent thinks he's beat either because he hasn't improved his hand or he thinks you have improved your hand.

It takes a lot of courage to fire a third barrel. Yet, it is a move that you should add into your game.

Here is how it works. You are the pre-flop raiser, and get one caller. You bet the flop with nothing, and get called. You bet the turn with nothing, and get called. When the river card comes, you still have nothing. But you fire that third barrel and hope.

Example:

You have 9♠-8♦ on the cut-off. It is the middle of the tournament. You have $44,000. The blinds are $400-$800. Everyone folds to you. You raise to $3,200. Only the player on the button, with $40,000, calls your bet. The pot is $7,600.

The flop is 7♠-6♦-2♦. You bet $5,000. Your opponent calls. The pot is $17,600. You have $35,800. Your opponent has $31,800.

The turn is a Q♥. You fire a second barrel and bet $10,000. Your opponent calls. The pot is $37,600. You have $25,800. Your opponent has $21,800. Feeling ill?

The river is a K♠. What should you do?

Your opponent called your bet when a scare card hit the turn. So maybe he hit top pair on the turn. But when the King hits on the river, it's another scare card. Since many players put their opponent on A-K when they raise pre-flop, you may win by firing a third barrel.

Fire the third barrel. Move all-in.

You move all-in. Your opponent thinks for a long time before he calls, and shows A♣-Q♣ to win the pot. Even though you lost this time, this is a gutsy and worthwhile move.

River Moves: The Naked Ace Bluff

91. Use the Naked Ace Bluff Move.

As mentioned earlier, the naked Ace bluff is when you are holding the Ace that is the same suit as the three cards on the board, and you use this information to bet as if you have the nut flush. Since your opponent knows he doesn't have the nut flush, he folds.

Example:

You have 6♥-6♦. It is the middle of the tournament. You have $18,000. The blinds are $150-$300. You raise under-the-gun to $800. Only the big blind, with $15,000, calls your bet. The pot is $1,750.

The flop is Q♥-4♥-2♥. The big blind check to you. You check, since you will have to fold to a check-raise and want a free card for your flush.

The turn is J♦. The big blind checks again. Now your pair is worse than before. You don't want to build a pot with third best pair, and a potential flush on board.

The river is the 6♠. The big blind bets $1,000. What should you do?

This looks like a blocking bet. You raise to $3,000.

The big blind re-raises to $10,000. What should you do?

There is now $15,750 in the pot. If you call this bet and lose, you will be left with $7,200. You fold.

Your opponent shows you the A♥, before he mucks. Was he using the naked Ace bluff move here? Or did he flop the nuts?

River Moves: Picking Off a Bluff

92. Some pointers on how to pick off bluffs on the river.

Sometimes a player will make a bet at the river that feels wrong. It may be that the player has not shown any strength and yet when a rag hits the river, he bets big. Or it may be that he has been check-calling your bets, but on the river he leads out with a small bet.

Of course, some players can make daring bluffs on the river. He may check-raise or even re-raise your raise. Those are not semi-bluffs! Your opponent either has the nuts or he is pulling off a great move. It is a strong player who can use a check-raise bluff on the river.

Sometimes a player will pause at the river for a long time before making a sizeable bet. This is often a tell that a player is acting weak when he is strong. This happens often online, where the lead bettor has been betting at an even pace until the river card. Now, you sit and wait and wait, until he finally makes his bet. He has a monster. Don't call.

The things to review at the river are an opponent's betting patterns, his tendency to bluff, and any tells. It takes time to learn when an opponent is bluffing, but trust your instincts when your opponent's actions don't feel right. You can call or even try to raise him off his hand.

Example:

You have A♠-K♠. It is the middle of the tournament. You have $20,000. The blinds are $300-$600. You raise to $2,4000 in an early position. Everyone folds to the big blind. He calls. He has $15,000. The pot is $5,100.

The flop is J♦-8♦-2♥. You missed. You bet $3,000. Your opponent calls. The pot is $11,100.

The turn is a 6♣. You missed again. You don't want to make this a bigger pot with an Ace-high hand. You figure you are beat, so you check. Your opponent checks.

The river is a 6♠. You check. Your opponent moves all-in for $9,600. What should you do?

This bet doesn't feel right. If your opponent had a hand, why didn't he bet the turn? This looks like a delayed river bluff.

You call. Your opponent shows the K♦-Q♦. You win a nice pot.

Heads-Up Moves: Eight to Live By

93. Position is critical in heads-up play, so at least call with any hand from the small blind/button.

The small blind/button has position from the flop on, and has a big advantage. Don't fold when you are the first to act. If your opponent folds too often from the small blind, he is playing to lose.

94. Try to figure out what your opponent is thinking, and his playing style.

Pay attention to how your opponent is playing. Since most players don't have a lot of experience heads-up, they tend to be consistent in their playing style. In fact, early in the match with a small pot, you should consider calling your opponent down with any pair if it will help you determine how he approaches heads-up play.

95. Vary your play. Don't play too weak or too strong. Don't play predictable poker.

Predictable poker simply signals to your opponent the strength of your hand by folding your bad hands, calling with your good hands, and raising with your premium hands.

Vary your play. You need to keep your opponent off-balance. You need to balance your moves so an opponent can't be sure if you are bluffing, strong, betting second pair, etc.

96. Flopping any pair is a strong hand heads-up.

If your opponent checks on the flop, bet with a pair. If your opponent bets, you should call and see what he does on the turn. Will he fire a second barrel or check and let you win with a bet?

97. If you are in the big blind with a garbage hand, and your opponent raises, you should just fold.

You don't want to play bad hands out of position. Of course, if your opponent raises you on a regular basis from the small blind/button, you need to take action; that is, determine if you want to call him down or playback at him. You can't let your opponent play too strong, or have him think you are too weak.

98. If your opponent consistently makes min-sized bets, don't fold your hand. Figure out if you want to raise his bets or try a delayed bluff.

When you check your hand and show weakness, some players will automatically make a play for the pot. They will make the smallest bet possible hoping you'll fold. If you call, and they don't improve, they will check in position. Check-raise or bet into them on the next street.

99. Don't overplay your strong hands out of position.

When your opponent raises in the small blind, don't re-raise with strong hands that need to improve. If you miss the flop, you are out of position and have put yourself in a tough situation in a big pot.

100. Try to pick off bluffs.

When you play against an aggressive opponent, you want to let him bet off his chips. He can't always have a big hand. Even if you have second pair, if you are in position, just call him down. It is tough to do, but it can win you a big pot. And if you have top pair, it is even an easier call to make.

TIP: Online Poker and Heads-Up Play

If you play online, don't compete against the players who sit and wait for victims at heads-up tables. These players are heads-up specialists. Get practice at the lower levels before you challenge the heads-up specialists.

Final Move:
Don't Let a Bad Beat Lead to Tilt

101. Take a break when you sense you are about to go on tilt.

This may be the most important move of all. Sometimes in poker you will experience a bad beat, or make a bad decision that costs you a lot of chips. You are human and you will internalize this loss. When you feel irritated, angry or even stupid, just walk away from the poker table and take a break.

When you're steaming about a previous hand, you can't be at your best. Even though every player knows this fact, they stay at the table and compound the last loss with a bad play. Tilt!

Don't go on tilt. It will be your worst and most costly decision in poker.

How To Put This Book Into Action

There are 101 moves in this book so I know it's impossible to add them all into your poker game today. But let me suggest how to approach improving your no-limit tournament game using these moves:

Use Chunking.

Learn these moves in chunks. Select a few moves and try them in your next tournament. Perhaps you start with two or three moves from pre-flop and flop play, and one or two moves from turn and river play. The idea is to make it easier to learn these moves by learning a few moves at a time.

See how the first chunk of moves works for you. If you like a move, keep using it. If you don't like it, put it aside for now.

Now add in another chunk of moves. Test them out and see how they work.

Keep repeating, until you have used them all. Even if you have only mastered a few moves your game will improve. You may become aware of the moves being used against you, so you can be successful at countermeasures.

The important part is to always strive not just to learn more, but also to put the learning into action. Chunking your learning makes it easier and as a result, you will win more often. Learn, experiment, and repeat. Best of all, cash out a winner.

Free updates: *To continue to help you improve your game, this book will be updated periodically. If you'd like to receive these free updates, please go to www.apokerexpert.com and click on the "contact us" page. On the "contact us" page, please type in your email address along with words "free updates." Any past and future updates to this book will be emailed to you for free.*

In addition, if you would like to provide input on any of the moves in this book or submit new moves, please submit them to me at: www.pokerexpert.com or to my email: mitch@apokerexpert.com. Thanks.

The Main Event:
You Versus a Champ Named Phil

Imagine...you did it! You made it to the final table of the WSOP Main Event. You are heads-up against some poker champ named Phil, playing for the $10 million first place prize money. While you already have the $5 million second place prize money, it would be a whole lot sweeter to take home the bracelet as the best player in the world.

Phil and you both have $20 million in chips.

It's the first hand of heads-up play. The blinds are $50,000-$100,000. You are in the big blind. Phil is on the button.

The cards are dealt. Phil raises to $500,000. You peek at your cards. Lousy hand. 10♣-7♥.

The lights are bright. Your adrenaline is flowing, but you're exhausted. You've been playing almost non-stop for days. You're in a haze. Is this a dream?

You know Phil is testing you. He wants to outmuscle you. He exudes confidence and cockiness. It's as if he's won a few times before. Oh yeah, right, he has.

You realize you can't outplay Phil. Your only defense is the all-in move against the Pro.

"All-in," you declare.

"He's going all-in on the first hand!" shouts the tournament director.

The sound of applause filters through your haze. You know there's a huge crowd that surrounds you, but you can no longer focus past the chairs that circle the table.

Phil is beside himself. "What's that? That's a bush league move! You want to play cards or what?" Phil tosses his hand away.

You breathe a sign of relief while raking in a half million of Phil's chips.

The second hand is dealt.

You act first and look down at 7♣-6♣. You limp in for $50,000.

Phil stands up, and playing to the crowd, shouts, "I'm all-in."

You are startled. You focus on Phil. The crowd is white noise.

Phil taunts you. "How do you like them apples? Two can play that game."

You laugh and fold. Phil holds his cards high in the air for all to see: 7♥-2♦.

The noise rises to a new level. Phil takes his bows, before settling down for the next hand.

The third hand is dealt.

You're back in the big blind, as you anxiously wait for the cards to come. Phil calls from the small blind.

You suddenly recall a move you read in the book *101 Winning Hold'em Moves*. The "no-look" blind steal. Without looking at your cards, you push all-in again.

You've barely finished when Phil yells "call!" and shoves his chips into the middle, making a mess. He flips his hole cards.

The tournament director announces, "Phil shows pocket 9's."

You know the crowd is going crazy, but you don't hear them at all.

You just stare at Phil's two black 9's. You are sick to your stomach. What a stupid play on your part!

"C'mon, show already?" Phil urges you to open your cards.

You reply sheepishly, "I haven't looked yet."

The announcer moves up next to you and asks, "What?"

You repeat the words into his microphone, "I haven't looked yet."

The announcer states to the crowd, "He moves all-in with $10 million on the line without looking. That's unreal!"

You flip the first card over….it's the Ace of hearts.

You flip the second card … the King of hearts.

It's a race.

"Idiots! I play against idiots who don't know what they're doing!" Yes, that's Phil again.

The dealer turns over the first three cards….they help no one.

Phil stands over the table, eager for his next bracelet.

You just sit, and hope.

The turn card is dealt...no help again.

Phil is ready to celebrate.

The river card. The Ace of spades!

You jump for joy! Phil moves next to you and shakes your hand.

$10 million and you owe it all to *101 Winning Hold'em Moves.*

Would you mind sending me 10%?

Appendix
Most Frequently Asked Poker Questions

A. Pre-flop questions

How often will I be dealt pocket Aces?
Once every 221 hands.

If my starting hand is not a pair, how often will I flop a pair to one of my cards?
32% of the time. This means the flop will miss your hand 68% of the time.

If my starting hand is a pair, how often will I flop a set or better?
About 12% of the time. This means you will make a set or better on the flop roughly one in eight times.

If I hold two suited cards, how often will I flop a draw to my flush?
About 11% of the time.

How often will I flop a straight draw?
Connected cards with zero gap and maximum stretch, such as J-T, will flop an open-ended straight draw about 10% of the time.
One-gapped connectors, such as 7-5, will flop an open ended-straight draw about 6% of the time.

If I have A-K as my starting hand, how often will I flop top pair or better?
33% of the time

What if my A-K is suited—how often will I flop top pair or better?
About 40% of the time

What is the probability of my A-K beating Q-Q? How much better is it if it's suited?

A-K offsuit wins 43% of the pots in head-to-head contests.

A-K suited wins 46% of the pots in head-to-head contests.

If I have a bigger pocket pair than my opponent, how big of a favorite am I?

You will win almost 80% of the time in a head-to-head contest.

If my opponent holds my highest card with a better kicker, how far ahead is he?

He is normally better than a 2 to 1 favorite to win the pot in a head-to-head contest.

What's the probability of my opponent having an Ace-high hand with a better kicker than me?

In an eight-handed game, if you hold A-J it's 13%, A-10 is 19%, A-9 is 24%, and A-8 is 30%.

How often will I flop two pair if my starting hand is not a pair?

About 2% of the time.

If my starting hand is a pair, what's the probability a player at my table will have a higher pair? For example, what if I have pocket Kings?

If you have pocket Kings, and you have 9 opponents, the probability one of your opponents has pocket Aces is about 4.5%. To get a rough estimate, take the number of higher pairs than the one you hold, multiply it by the number of your opponents, and divide by 2. That's the probability that there will be at least one higher pair.

B. Flop questions

What are "outs"?

Outs are the number of cards available to complete your draw or make a specific hand.

What is the fastest way to estimate the probability of making my draw on the turn and/or the river?

From the flop to the turn, or the turn to the river: Take the number of outs and multiply it by 2 to get the probability. Example: If you have 8 outs on the flop, it is 8 x 2 = 16% of the time you will complete your draw on the turn.

From the flop to the river: Take the number of outs and multiply it by 4 to get the probability. Example: If you have 8 outs on the flop, it is 8 x 4 = 32% of the time you will complete your draw on the river.

(See footnote 1)

How are probabilities and odds different?

Probabilities are the % of the time you will end up with a desired hand.

Odds in poker mean the odds against improving to a desired hand.

Example: You flop a straight draw that gives you 8 outs. Your probability of making a straight with two cards to come is 32%. The odds are 2 to 1 (against improving to a straight with two cards to come).

(See footnote 2 for formula on how to convert probabilities to odds)

How many outs do I need on the flop to be the favorite, if I play to the river?

With 13 outs you have odds of 48.1% to make your hand on the river.

With 14 outs you have odds of 51.2% to make your hand on the river.

With 15 outs you have odds of 54.1% to make your hand on the river.

How often will I make my flush when I flop a four card flush draw?
About 36% of the time

How often will I make my straight when I flop a four card straight draw?
About 32% of the time

If the flop does not contain a pair, how often will it be paired if the cards go to the river?
About 40% of the time.

How often will two or three cards of the same suit flop?
About 55% of the time.

3. Complaints:

Why do I lose with pocket Jacks all the time?
Your Jacks are vulnerable since a card higher than a Jack will flop over 65% of the time.

How come my A-Q always runs into A-K?
The probability that an opponent has A-K when you hold A-Q is just 7% in an eight-handed game. However, assuming you made a pre-flop raise, your opponent will need a strong hand to compete. This is where probability meets reality—the reality is that you run into A-K more often since it's one of the common hands opponents will play against your pre-flop raise.

How low should my chip stack be when it's simply best to move all-in pre-flop, rather than make a standard three times big blind raise?
When your chip stack is less than 9 times the big blind.

Why did my A-K starting hand lose to 2-2?
2-2 wins 53% of the pots in head-to-head contests.

Why did my J-10 suited starting hand lose to A-K?
> A-K wins 59% of the pots in head-to-head contests.

Why did my 2-2 starting hand lose to J-10 suited?
> J-10 suited wins 53% of the pots in head-to-head contests.

Is there a trick to putting my opponent on a hand?
> Experience is the key as it will help you to determine the hands an opponent will play pre-flop and what hands he is likely to hold if he continues to play after seeing the flop cards.

How come I get so many bad beats?
> It happens to everyone. Luck is part of the game. Remember, "Bad beats only happen to good players." -- Joe Crow (1998)
>
> If you have the best hand of pocket Aces, and move all-in pre-flop against your opponent's hand of 7-2 (considered the weakest hand in poker), you will lose more than once in every nine hands. And, if your pocket Aces is all-in pre-flop against any pocket pair, you will lose more than 20% of the time. Any two cards can win.

How come the probabilities never work out for me-- I lose a lot more often than what the probabilities say I should?
> In no-limit poker, probabilities meet reality. While you need to know the basic probabilities, the reality is that your opponents will be competing against you in raised pots with strong hands. Therefore, in raised pots, the universe of potential hands is reduced significantly, and you face a smaller, stronger set of hands.

How come I never win?
> You haven't put *Tournament Poker: 101 Winning Moves* into action.

Footnote 1: To get a more accurate probability using the number of outs:

On a card-by-card basis: The multiple is 2.2
From the flop to the river: The multiple is 4 for up to 9 outs, and 3.8 if you have 10 or more outs)

Footnote 2: To convert probabilities to odds you subtract the probability, expressed as a percentage, from 100 and divide the result by the probability. Example: Two cards to make the straight is 32%: (100-32) divided by 32 = roughly 2 to 1)

Sources:
The Science of Poker, by Dr. Mahmood N. Mahmood
Cardplayer.com, Texas Hold'em Odds Calculator

Appendix
Planning: Boring But Necessary

A) *Plan before the event starts*:

How fast is the tournament given the buy-in, chips, time limits and number of players?

Do you have the time needed to commit 100% to the event?

Are you rested so you can make the right decisions?

Are there are other things on your mind that will distract your attention and affect your play?

Are you going to go into the event being aggressive or passive? Or, are you going to let the cards determine your play at the start?

B) *Plan Your Hand Before the Cards are Dealt*:

What is your position at the table?

What is your chip stack relative to the big blinds?

Who are the players in the blinds, and do they defend their blinds?

What is your table image?

What is your chip stack relative to the players behind you?

What action has occurred in front of you?

What types of players have entered the pot; that is, what are their table images?

Has someone taken a bad beat that will effect how he plays this hand?

Has a new player been added to your table, or has a player been knocked out? If so, will that change the way the table plays?

C) Plan Your Hand When You Decide to Enter the Pot

1. Questions to think about pre-flop:
   What range of hands do you put your opponents on who entered the pot?
   Do you want action on the hand? Or do you want to raise to end the action?
   How much should you bet to accomplish your objective?
   What will you do if your opponent calls or raises your bet?

2. Questions to think about before the cards hit the flop:
   What range of hands do you put your opponents on given the pre-flop action?
   How big is the pot?
   How many opponents are in the hand?
   How many chips does your opponent have?
   What is your position relative to your opponents?
   What are your opponents' table images? And how does their chip stacks affect their decisions?
   What is your opponents' view of your table image?
   Don't forget that your opponents have a view on your style that will influence their decisions. Don't make the mistake to think that all your opponents have the same image of your play.

3. Questions to think about when the flop hits:
   Do you have the best hand, a drawing hand or nothing?
   Did this flop help or hurt my opponent's hand?
   What type of flop is this? What kind of opportunities or threats does it pose for your hand?
   Do you want to keep this a small pot or have it become a big pot?

4. Repeat for turn and river play

Chart: Odds Against Improving

Outs	Flop: Odds Against Improving on Turn	Turn: Odds Against Improving on River	Flop: Odds Against Improving when All-in on Flop
1 Out	46.0 to 1	45.0 to 1	22.5 to 1
2 Outs	22.5 to 1	22.0 to 1	10.9 to 1
3 Outs	14.7 to 1	14.3 to 1	7.0 to 1
4 Outs	10.8 to 1	10.5 to 1	5.1 to 1
5 Outs	8.4 to 1	8.2 to 1	3.9 to 1
6 Outs	6.8 to 1	6.7 to 1	3.1 to 1
7 Outs	5.7 to 1	5.6 to 1	2.6 to 1
8 Outs	4.9 to 1	4.8 to 1	2.2 to 1
9 Outs	4.2 to 1	4.1 to 1	1.9 to 1
10 Outs	3.7 to 1	3.6 to 1	1.6 to 1
11 Outs	3.3 to 1	3.2 to 1	1.4 to 1
12 Outs	2.9 to 1	2.8 to 1	1.2 to 1
13 Outs	2.6 to 1	2.5 to 1	1.1 to 1
14 Outs	2.4 to 1	2.3 to 1	1.0 to 1
15 Outs	2.1 to 1	2.1 to 1	0.8 to 1
16 Outs	1.9 to 1	1.9 to 1	0.8 to 1
17 Outs	1.8 to 1	1.7 to 1	0.7 to 1
18 Outs	1.6 to 1	1.6 to 1	0.6 to 1
19 Outs	1.5 to 1	1.4 to 1	0.5 to 1
20 Outs	1.4 to 1	1.3 to 1	0.5 to 1
21 Outs	1.2 to 1	1.2 to 1	0.4 to 1
22 Outs	1.1 to 1	1.1 to 1	0.4 to 1

New! Now you can get poker insurance with PokerSurance.

Does your online site include PokerSurance?

You've seen poker professionals on TV buy insurance when they move all-in on a hand of poker. It's a smart bet since it protects them from a bad beat and losing all their money. But, everyday players don't have this option and experience the real pain of going broke.

A new side bet called PokerSurance™ gives every poker player the insurance option formerly reserved only for high-limit poker pros.

Here's a typical example:

You move all-in with pocket Aces and get called by another player's inferior hand. But, the poker gods are against you and your aces get cracked. You are busted and leave a loser.

With a PokerSurance bet, when you are all-in, the dealer offers you PokerSurance. Now, if you lose to this player's inferior hand, you still win your PokerSurance bet. You play longer, and win more.

While poker insurance has been around for decades, it was something negotiated on the side between the high rollers of poker. Casinos didn't offer it to their players since they never figured out how to make money on it.
A PokerSurance bet solves the problem as it sets up a consistent way for the dealer to offer an attractive wager for players.

PokerSurance is available for on-line poker sites, casinos and card rooms. Ask your online poker site to include PokerSurance in their games today.

To find out more about PokerSurance, contact mcogert@gmail.com.

Razz Poker is the easiest way to consistently win money at poker. It is the one remaining game where the knowledge base remains small because most players have climbed on the bandwagon of the bigger and better known games. Yet, to win at Razz poker and in the "R" in HORSE poker, you need to know what the other players still don't.

Play Razz Poker to Win is going to give you that winning edge. It reveals new strategies that are proven to work since they are based on probabilities, hand simulations and actual play.

In *Play Razz Poker to Win*, you'll discover:

> The new Starting Hand Point System that shows you how to determine the strength of your hand taking into account your position, the exposed cards on board, and the betting action of the players.

> How to steal the antes by taking advantage of both passive and aggressive players.

> A new strategy for 4th street play when you hit a mediocre or bad card, called the Two-Level Rule

> Proof that the best drawing hand after five cards is <u>not</u> always the favorite over an already made 9 low!

> The right way to decide how to play your hand on 5th street; it's not as simple as the best hand versus best draw.

> Why 6th street is often about knowing the numbers 7-1.

> How being a calling station is not a bad concept for 7th street.

Over 100 Razz poker hand examples that put these strategies into action.

Buy *Play Razz Poker to Win* today and be a consistent winner at poker...Razz poker.